Lift the Label

Lift the Label

Esther Stansfield
David Westlake

10 09 08 07 06 05 04   7 6 5 4 3 2 1

First published 2004 by Spring Harvest Publishing Division and
Authentic Media
9 Holdom Avenue, Bletchley, Milton Keynes, Bucks, MK1 1QR, UK
and Box 1047, Waynesboro, GA 30830-2047
www.authenticmedia.co.uk

British Library Cataloguing in Publication Data
A catalogue record for this book is available from the British Library

ISBN 1-85078-572-4

Cover design by Peter Barnsley
Print Management by Adare Carwin

Thanks to all at Authentic Media and Spring Harvest, especially Steve May Miller, Charlotte Hubback, and Sam Redwood, for gladly giving us the opportunity to put our passion onto paper, and for being so great to work with.

We are also really grateful to Chantal Finney and Sam Maher at Labour Behind the Label; Sarah Garden at Fairtrade Foundation; and Pins Brown and Julia Hawkins at Ethical Trading Initiative for your help and advice. Many thanks to Craig Borlaise, Catherine Thomas and Liz Jennings for permitting us to use extracts from their feature articles in Tearfund's 'Uncovered' magazine.

Special thanks goes to Stephanie Dennison, and our colleagues at Tearfund, Dewi Hughes, Stephen Rand, Nigel Taylor, Zoe Hayes and the youth team, for your invaluable input, wise advice, inspiration, and rapid response chocolate provision throughout the birthing process! We are especially grateful to Tearfund's youth team for your willingness to create space to enable us to pursue this project.

To Ben – my rock. For your incredible love, unshakeable faith, inspiring vision and Christ-like heart. Thank you.
To Mum, Dad and family – for your unfailing love and care, and for showing me Jesus. Thank you.

Esther

To Minu- who inspires me, keeps me honest and teaches me the meaning of love.
To Ellie – who makes me want to seek the kingdom more than ever.

David

Contents

One

It's Amazing What You Don't See

'Here is Edward Bear coming down the stairs now, bump, bump, bump, bump on the back of his head. It is, as far as he knows, the only way of coming down the stairs but sometimes he feels there really is another way, if he could only stop bumping for a moment and think of it.'

A.A. Milne, from Winnie the Pooh

I couldn't wait to get to the guest house. It was hot and we had just arrived in Kampala having spent a long day driving across the Ugandan countryside. As I climbed the hill I saw a motel-like building and breathed a sigh of relief. 'It's modern. It's clean. There will be hot water. It will have fans in the rooms – or even air conditioning.' After the long, hot journey my heart leapt.

It's amazing what you don't see.

I didn't see that behind the modern building, just by the church, was another building – the old guesthouse. There were no fans and limited hot water. Just as I arrived, the electricity failed and so the place was lit with candles. 'But at least it is clean,' I thought to myself as I looked into my room.

You need to know that I am a bit funny about nature. Actually, I am very funny about bugs. I really am not good with anything that has more legs than me ... or fur ... or wings ... or is very small ... or very big. Don't get me wrong, I really like the idea of nature as a concept, but I

1

truly dislike nature when it is sharing a bedroom with me. So, when I'm staying in a dodgy guest house in the developing world, I thoroughly check the room.

It's amazing what you don't see.

When I went to sleep, the room was clean and lovely. I was alone. When I awoke the next morning, there was a cockroach on my pillow, looking right back at me. Glancing down, I saw that the floor was covered in cockroaches. I then looked down the bed. The whole sheet was covered with small red insects. They were all looking at me, hungrily.

It's amazing what you don't see.

There were lots of people staying in the guest house. One of them, a bishop from Rwanda, was travelling with his family. I got chatting to him one night. I was fascinated by his story. I was fascinated by his country.

In the 90s, 80% of Rwandans would have described themselves as Christian. I wanted to hear what it was like to live and serve God in such a context.

We know Rwanda for another reason – the civil war of the early 1990s, which brought the word genocide back into modern use. The reasons for the war were, inevitably, complex but, basically, the long running animosity between Hutu and Tutsi escalated into bloodshed and violence. No one knows how many died – maybe one million, according to some estimates. Communities were torn apart. Looting and pillaging became widespread and rape commonplace and all in a place regarded as Christian.

The bishop was a broken man. He had suffered greatly. He had chosen to stay with his people, doing what he could to protect people from both sides. He had gone with his flock into a refugee camp. He was a faithful shepherd.

He talked about Rwanda in the good days – the crowds coming to church and the thousands who were saved. Then his mood changed. He became very sad. 'We made a mistake,' he said. 'We taught the people about having their sins forgiven and going to heaven. We never taught them that hatred in your heart for another would separate you from God. We never challenged the racism and fear in our society.' After a quiet pause he continued, 'And when the enemy came, he found much in us to use.'

It's amazing what you don't see.

Despite all the blessings of God and demonstrations of his presence, despite the crowds and the services, the Rwandans had just not seen that hatred and racism would open up a way for the

What is our blind spot?

enemy to come and destroy people's lives, and set back God's work. They were busy doing all that they knew, they were busy doing all that they had been taught, but they had a blind spot. There was an area that mattered intensely to God that they had not addressed. They just hadn't seen its importance.

It took me a long time to get the point. I started off amazed that they could have neglected such basic teaching as 'loving your neighbour'. Then the penny dropped. If they, in their culture, had ended up with such a huge blind spot, what about me, in my culture?

I have been going to church since I was three years old. What had been missed out in all my discipleship and Bible studies and conferences? Where was my blind spot? What are the things that Christians in the West don't talk about? What do we treat as optional for the really keen ones? What is it that we are missing that is actually incredibly important to God? What is our blind spot?

It's amazing what you don't see.

I live a long way from Kampala, but the bishop's story still haunts me. As I grew up as a Christian, I learned the

Bible stories and was taught the importance of family and sexual morality. I learned that God cared about unborn children and the unsaved millions. I learned that as a Christian I should pray, be kind and give my money to support God's work and those in need. I learned all these things, but I never knew what I was missing.

All those things are true. But it is amazing what you don't see.

I was never told that God wanted to do something to stop people being poor. I was never told that it pains God when people are living at subsistence levels and have to fight just to survive. I was never told that he commands us to act in his name on their behalf. No one ever asked me how I spend my money. We talked about 'how far' a Christian could go with their girlfriend or boyfriend. We never talked about whether Jesus would buy a £40,000 four-wheel drive car. We gave money to famine relief and filled lorries with clothes. We never asked whether our lifestyles helped keep people poor. We never thought that the way we spend our money could have great impact for good or ill on millions of people. We never thought it was *that* important to God. Discipleship, after all, is about Bible study, prayer, worship and evangelism.

I was never told that God wanted to do something to stop people being poor.

It's amazing what you don't see.

This book is about that blind spot. We are incredibly grateful for our Christian heritage. We have learned so much, experienced so much and received so much. But something is missing. There is an area of God's heart and biblical truth that we have underestimated, that we have put to one side and reserved for those who are interested.

This book is about exposing our blind spot. But that's not why we wrote it. It's about fighting poverty and seeking justice. But that's not why we wrote it. It's about explaining the links between our high street spending and some of the poorest people in the world. But that's not why we wrote it. It's about changing the world by improving the working conditions and prospects for millions of people. But that's not why we wrote it. It's about stopping abusive child labour, creating safe factories and ensuring fair wages. But that's not why we wrote it. We wrote this book because we want to follow Jesus.

We want to be faithful to Jesus and *all* of his teaching, not just the nice, comforting bits. We want to be faithful to the bits that challenge us, question us and cause us to struggle. We want to live the eternal kind of life. We want to start living it now by beginning to think as he thinks, feel as he feels and acting as he would act. We want to put away the blind spots we have inherited from our Western Christian upbringing.

We want to see.

This book takes you on a journey along the global roadside. We want you to meet our neighbours and uncover the reality of their lives. It is a call to look beyond the bargain to *see* the reality of what is happening behind the scenes when we shop. It's an invitation to listen to the people whose fingerprints are on the products that we buy. It's a challenge to *change* our habits to reflect God's heart for justice and mercy – even when we shop.

The book is divided into three sections. In the first, we are going to see the realities of the global garment and food industries. We will listen to the voices of people working to provide us with our food and clothes. Section Two will explore in more depth what the Bible teaches about our global neighbours and our responsibilities to them. Section

Three will discuss how to take action and live differently, so that we can follow Jesus and help our neighbours.

Section One

MEET THE NEIGHBOURS

Two

Who is My Neighbour?

"All knowledge should be translated into action."
Albert Einstein

A man met with Jesus and asked, 'What must I do to get eternal life?' Lots of people asked Jesus that question or one like it. They saw and heard and felt truth in him. Something that went beyond words and rules and tradition. Something that was real, vibrant and powerful. Mostly they were people who were doing the best they could. Doing everything their religion had taught them. But they were desperate for something different. Something real. Something eternal. You can almost hear the desperation in their voices, 'What must I do? I have tried everything I know. I am doing everything I know. But there must be more than this. There must be more than keeping rules and doing my best. Where is this eternal kind of life that I have dreamed of? How do I get it?'

The man I am thinking of asked his question in Luke chapter 10.

'What must I do to get eternal life?'

He was a religious expert and so they had a conversation about it all and decided that it was really easy. You just had to do two things: First love God with everything inside of you and secondly, love your neighbour as much as you love yourself.

Like most of the really fundamental truths it is really easy to understand but really hard to do. The man began to feel a bit silly and so he asked another question to try to show that it was all a bit more complicated. 'And who is my neighbour?'

Jesus answered by telling one of the most famous of his stories – the parable of the Good Samaritan.

Luke 10:30-37 (NIV)

[30] In reply Jesus said: "A man was going down from Jerusalem to Jericho, when he fell into the hands of robbers. They stripped him of his clothes, beat him and went away, leaving him half dead.

[31] A priest happened to be going down the same road, and when he saw the man, he passed by on the other side.

[32] So too, a Levite, when he came to the place and saw him, passed by on the other side.

[33] But a Samaritan, as he travelled, came where the man was; and when he saw him, he took pity on him.

[34] He went to him and bandaged his wounds, pouring on oil and wine. Then he put the man on his own donkey, took him to an inn and took care of him.

[35] The next day he took out two silver coins and gave them to the innkeeper. 'Look after him,' he said, 'and when I return, I will reimburse you for any extra expense you may have.'

[36] "Which of these three do you think was a neighbour to the man who fell into the hands of robbers?"

[37] The expert in the law replied, "The one who had mercy on him."

Jesus told him, "Go and do likewise."

I have been taught this story since the children's club at church. I have been told it, I have read it, and I have learned songs and drama sketches about it. The point has always been that I should be like the Good Samaritan. That I should do my 'good deed for the day' and that Christians should be kind to others. All of this is true. And none of it is why Jesus told the story.

Jesus is answering a specific question: 'What must I do to get eternal life?' The man was probably trying to trap him into saying something wrong so that the religious leaders could attack him. But maybe he was also intrigued, desperate even, for the answer.

They had already decided that the key issue in getting the eternal kind of life was love. Loving God and loving others. Jesus had already transformed people's understanding about loving God. Changing it from being about keeping rules to being about a living relationship. Moving it from being about a distant almighty God to being about an almighty God

Who is my neighbour? Whoever needs you to be.

who invites us to call him 'Father'. In this part of the Bible Jesus goes further. You cannot get the eternal kind of life simply by concentrating on your relationship with God. Your relationship with others is also vitally important. We have to love our neighbours.

Now this really scared the man. Talk about loving God was one thing. In his mind you did that in private. Praying, reading the Bible, meditating, keeping strict rules about food and dress codes. Or you did it in meetings where you worshipped and heard the Bible explained. Sure, you had to help people when you could, but it wasn't central. He probably thought about other people the most when he was trying to work out who was religious and who wasn't.

After all he was a religious leader. He couldn't be seen with 'unclean' people. He had standards.

'Love your neighbour as you love yourself.'

He panicked. 'What, everyone? Surely there must be some mistake. Just who exactly is my neighbour?'

And so Jesus told him the story.

A man is mugged and left for dead. Three people walk down the road where he is lying. Two of them are religious leaders. One is a despised foreigner, a Samaritan. Three people are walking down the road. Only one person sees who is there. The religious people are too busy, too self absorbed, too scared to stop and see. After all, they have important things to do. Lots of people get mugged on that road, and it really isn't safe to stop and get involved. Besides how do they know if the man lying there really is mugged? Is he just pretending, waiting for someone to stop so his friends can jump out and mug the new fool?

They don't see what is there. They don't stop. They don't see *who* is there.

Then along comes the Samaritan. The wrong person from the wrong race. Some of the people listening to Jesus tell this story probably spat, and groaned, and swore when he mentioned a Samaritan. Jews and Samaritans hated each other. 'That's right', they said. 'Trust a Samaritan to come along and gloat. Probably rob him again and finish him off. You know what Samaritans are like.'

Which is where Jesus astonished them. Again.

The Samaritan was the one who saw who was there. Lying by the road. In need. He was the one who did something. He gave him first aid. He took him to a place of safety. Paid his bills. He was a neighbour. The crowd would have fallen silent as Jesus not only told a story of great kindness but also challenged all their racist ideas about Samaritans.

He also completely turned around the concept of loving others. The religious leader had asked, 'Who is my neighbour?' At the end of the story Jesus asks him a question. 'Who was the neighbour?' The religious man wanted to limit the number of people he had to love. Jesus told him about a man who loved people simply because they needed love. The way to get the eternal kind of life, Jesus tells him, is to be a neighbour to everyone who needs a neighbour.

Being a neighbour cost the Samaritan time and money. It was inconvenient and expensive. Too inconvenient and expensive for the religious leaders. They passed by on the other side and missed the man lying by the road. They also missed out on the eternal kind of life.

We still ask the question 'Who is my neighbour?' The answer that comes back is still the same: 'Whoever needs you to be.' We still want to know the limits of our compassion – who do we have to love and who can we ignore? Jesus still points us to a better way.

We must show mercy to those who need mercy. Love to those who need love. Give service to those who are in need. This is being a neighbour. This is the path to the eternal kind of life.

We want you to meet some new neighbours. They are lying by the side of the road in need and yet we have often walked past them. We have hardly noticed them even though they impact every part of our lives every day.

Three

Beyond the Barcode

"Before you've finished your breakfast this morning,
you'll have relied on half the world."
Martin Luther King

Some neighbours are so close to us that we can't even see them.

You came into contact with your global neighbours even before leaving the house this morning. Your hands were not the first to touch your clothes. Today, as you got dressed, you put on clothes that have come to you via your neighbours around the world.

Despite being bought in local high street shops, your trainers may have been stitched in Indonesia, your hooded top in Bangladesh and jeans in Malaysia. The order may have been placed in Hong Kong, the cloth sourced from India, stitched in China and the buttons sewn on in the UK.

As you had a cup of coffee, glass of orange juice or a banana this morning, did you realise that the average breakfast has travelled 5000 miles to reach you?[1] Your orange juice, tea, coffee, bananas, sugar and honey have all passed through the hands of some of the world's poorest people before landing on your kitchen table.

The fingerprints of our global neighbours are all over our food and clothes. It is just that we can't see them. It is their hands that have plucked our bananas, picked our tea

leaves and collected our coffee beans. It is their fingers that
have stitched the seams onto our denim jackets, punched
the buttonhole into our jeans and glued the sole onto our
trainers. People, not
machines, carry out all
these jobs. These men,
women and children are
people who matter to
God. Their stories
deserve to be told. Every product we buy tells a story of a
person who has hopes, dreams and fears, just like us. By
buying their products we become part of their story.

*Every product we buy tells a story
of a person who has hopes, dreams
and fears just like us.*

That story can be shocking.

These people are usually among the most
disadvantaged, living in the world's poorest countries. Just
like the traveller on the road to Jericho, they are easy to
exploit, because they are desperate, needy and are not
powerful enough to stand up for themselves or protect their
own interests. They are in a weak and vulnerable position.
Busy people, like you and I, can choose to walk on by or
stop, take notice and do something to help.

Shima is one neighbour who, just like the traveller on
the road from Jerusalem to Jericho is vulnerable and in
need of someone to stop and care. I met Shima in
November 2002 when she was seventeen. She left school at
fourteen. It wasn't a choice. Her family was so poor they
couldn't afford to keep a growing girl who was doing no
more than studying. Just like the traveller, she left the
familiar territory of her school and home in the country and
went on a journey to seek a better life – to find employment
and a chance of providing for herself and her family.

In Dhaka, capital of Bangladesh, Shima found work in a
busy clothes factory, where she has been working for three
years.

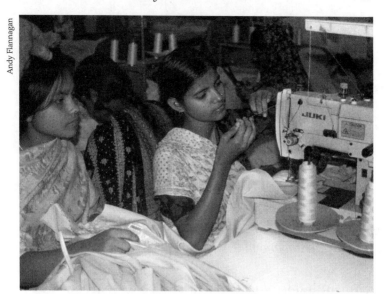

Andy Flannagan

Shima operating sewing machine, Bangladesh

The fans to cool the workers in Shima's factory are broken. The rubbish piles up on the window ledges. There is no fire equipment on the stairs. Her job is to stitch buttonholes on jeans and jackets. Many of the clothes she makes end up in UK stores. Shima works from 8 a.m. to 8 p.m. or 9 p.m., six days a week. After three years at the factory, she earns a grand weekly total of £4.40. She would need twice that amount just to afford basic essentials like nutritious food, adequate healthcare and accommodation. After work, Shima returns to her home in a dangerous slum area and sleeps. She has neither the time nor the money for anything else.

The slums in Dhaka are not a safe or healthy place to live. There are no proper toilet facilities. Piles of rotting rubbish and open sewers stagnate close to where children play and workers walk home from the factory. For women, especially, the risks are high. In a single month, thirty-one female garment workers were raped as they walked from their factory shifts to their home in the slums.[2] Public buses and rickshaws are a luxury their wages cannot stretch to. Shima says, 'This wage is not enough to live on, to have good food on, or to be able to afford to go out in town after work to relax.'[3]

Shima is not alone. She is one of 1.5 million employees in the garment industry in Bangladesh. Her clothes factory is one of 3,024 in the country. Of these workers, 80 per cent are women and, like her, are mainly between fourteen and twenty-nine years old. The average worker in the garment industry in Bangladesh has to share their low wage with five people who depend on them for financial support.[4]

'This wage is not enough to live on.' (Shima, garment worker)

Worldwide, 850 million workers are earning less than a living wage on which they can afford to feed their families, pay for medicines when they are ill or live in adequate accommodation.[5] Most of the workers in the garment industry are based in Asia, the Americas and Eastern Europe, with a significant number in Africa. However, there are garment workers located all across the world, including in the UK. Of the global garment industry workforce, 90 per cent are women, who mostly work in factories.[6] Many have no choice but to work long hours, six or even seven days a week, in unsafe and unhealthy conditions, sewing, stitching and gluing together the clothes which often end up on the shelves of high street shops in the USA, UK and Europe. For many it is the only way to survive. Others are home-workers, given work by factories, such as stitching buttons onto clothes, which they complete at home, from where it is collected. Most of these are women with caring responsibilities, so working at home is their only option for earning money. These women often face similar issues of exploitation, as the garment workers in factories, in terms of their low wages, long hours, and little or no rights to speak up about their situation.

The struggles of these people matter to God, and he wants them to matter to us. He knows the names of the 250 million children who work as child labourers instead of going to school.[7] These children do every job imaginable – including producing textiles, clothes, carpets, shoes and toys – and are often working in the most appalling conditions. Many of them die before they reach adulthood.

Far too many of the people who produce some of our food, sportswear, carpets and rugs, as well as electronic goods, are facing similar issues of exploitation and oppression. They make the products that make our lives possible.

Behind the Label

Our shopping is cold, impersonal and shrink-wrapped. It's hard enough to remember to smile at the person at the till, let alone think of someone thousands of miles away who made our jeans or picked our coffee. In our advertising-soaked consumer culture, most of the information about the things we buy comes directly from the companies that sell them. Before the average British child hits primary school they will have seen 30,000 adverts.[8] It's easy to be blinded by the dazzling lights and stimulating slogans of the adverts, as they tell us only what the company wants us to know. We rarely find out about the reality behind the products they are promoting. It's hard to stop and look beyond the bargain price tag when we shop. But how would things change if we were to lift the label on our food jars or clothing and found the reality of the life of the person who made the product?

What if the label also told us what it had cost the person who made it? What was the price in terms of *their* time, *their* energy, *their* family life, *their* stress levels, *their* physical condition, *their* hopes and dreams? Would we shop differently? Would we still have bought the same pair of jeans if Shima's story were on the label?

Take a moment to lift the care label on one item of clothing that you are wearing right now. It will probably tell you how to care for that jumper or top, when to dry clean only, or hand wash. It doesn't tell you how the person who made the item was treated – the hours they worked, the wages they received and the conditions they worked in.

The lives and situations of our global neighbours are virtually invisible. They are hidden behind the brand name and the packaging. It is not Shima's face that will be splashed across company adverts on billboards or on TV. She will not be seen walking down the catwalks in London, Milan, or New York fashion week. Her name will not be filling up the column inches in the glossy fashion magazines. Her photo will not be dominating the window displays on the high street. Her face will not be enlarged in the aisle during the promotional week at the supermarket.

These neighbours are the hidden people. They live hidden lives, out of the spotlight, lying on the global roadside. Out of sight and out of mind for the busy consumer on the bustling high street rushing for a bargain.

What if the labels on our clothes, food and other products told us this information about the people who supplied them? Would we shop differently?

Four

Clothes to Die For

'Never doubt that a small group
of committed citizens can change the world.
Indeed, it is the only thing that ever has.'
Margaret Mead, US Anthropologist

Rokye is a young man, in his early twenties, with dark shiny hair and bright eyes. When I met him, he was sitting cross-legged and bare-footed, on top of a long bench, in a busy clothes factory in Dhaka city, Bangladesh. Rokye looked uncomfortable. He was hunched over something, his back bent, frantically moving his fingers backwards and forwards. There was no chair for him to sit on, so he couldn't change position if he had a sore back or began to hurt. As I moved closer I could see what he was working on. It was a denim jacket. On it he was sewing small, sparkly, diamante beads, one by one. He had to hold the material up close to his eyes to see what he was doing. Each bead was small and had to be threaded first and then sewn on to the jacket. There was no break when he finished one jacket. He just picked up another one and started all over again.

His manager proudly called it 'the 315 jacket', because of the number of hand sewn diamante beads on it. Rokye repeats the same painstaking threading and sewing action 315 times on each jacket. His yellowed nails, bruised from the needles, show how hard he works. Everyone in the factory works hard. Large orders require fast work. In this factory, the number of clothes produced every day is around 15,000. The workers have to work so fast that they often cut themselves on the needles. Rokye is surrounded by lots of other workers, all repeating their individual tasks, all day long.

He can't afford a cinema ticket or a bus journey out of the city.

Shamin punches the button holes in the denim and Bithe pops on the metal rings around the punched hole. Halida cuts the threads off the completed jackets and Hachem irons them. Finally Beauty attaches the label tags.

All of them sit close together but they are not allowed to talk as they carry out their tedious routine. The workers are only allowed to break their silence when the managers speak to them.

Rokye's story is not unusual in clothes factories. I visited one which had signs on the walls saying, 'NO TALK, ONLY DO YOUR WORK', and 'HARD LABOUR IS THE KEY TO SUCCESS.' In some factories in Bangladesh, workers can even be forced to pay a fine out of their already poor wages, if they are caught talking while at work.

Rokye usually works from 8am until 8pm. However, he said that he often worked until 1am, and sometimes until 3am or 4am as a double shift, with only one break. I imagined that such intricate and highly skilled work would at least command a decent pay packet at the end of the month. This is not the case. Rokye earns around 1400 taka per month – a grand total of £20. This wage is not enough for him to have a reasonable quality of life. The food that he, and most workers, can afford on this salary is not good. They usually don't have breakfast, and eat only a very basic lunch and dinner – mainly rice – with maybe fish or meat as a luxury just once a week. He can't afford a cinema ticket

Andy Flannagan

The '315' diamante jacket

or a bus journey out of the city. There is no opportunity for leisure activities and little chance of having a social life. They spend most of their time working. They hardly see the city or their homes in daylight hours. To make matters worse, pay is often not paid on time and many workers have to wait up to two months to receive it. To live properly Rokye needs twice the current amount. That would just make it possible to afford the basics of food, accommodation and medicine.

Rokye and most of the other garment factory workers rent a room in the Dhaka slums that surround the factories. Usually, five or six workers share a cramped space together. In the area where he lives, the poverty statistics are shocking. A staggering 64 per cent of people are malnourished, 85 per cent of the houses have no electricity and the infant mortality rate in the slums is double the already high national average.[9] There is a stench from the piles of rotting rubbish in the area. The children play and dogs bark beside the open sewers. The alleys are full of stagnant pools of water with dark clouds of mosquitoes hovering menacingly overhead. There is very poor sanitation and hygiene here making diarrhoea common, as well as potentially fatal diseases such as malaria. Most people in the area have no running water. They are forced to get their water from wells and ponds that are unclean and often carry disease. Residents have to pay for clean water from the water authority. That is another 200 taka a month. Garment workers like Rokye who earn 1400 taka a month can't afford it.

Rokye's story is echoed by many garment workers worldwide, who are struggling to provide for themselves and their families.

In Cambodia, for example, a 22-year-old woman called Vanna, gathers and prepares cloth for the sewing machine in a busy garment factory. She has worked in this factory for eight years, since she was 14 years old. This is when her parents, who were desperately poor, had no choice but to send Vanna to work, and her mother was forced to change her age on their family's identity card to show her as 18 years old. Vanna's diary does not reflect the busy social whirl of that of a typical 22-year-old in the UK. On a usual week her diary will be blocked out from 7am to 7pm, Monday to Saturday with the word WORK, and in that daily period she can rest for only one hour. This relentless work is rewarded by a mere £13.50 wage per month, making it hard to afford even the bare essentials.

'The managers of this factory are very hard and strict.'
Vanna, garment worker

Vanna, who is a Christian, says, 'sometimes I work until the morning. The managers of this factory are very hard and strict, not thinking about the rights or plight of the workers. A safe working environment, breaks, benefits, and a fair salary are far from their thinking. I only have Sunday mornings to go to church.'

Vanna longs to have the time and energy to have fun with her church youth group friends. She dreams of finishing her education, going to college and working with an organisation that has good working conditions, fair wages, and which gives her enough time to serve in her church.

'All that is necessary for evil to triumph is for good men to do nothing.' Edmund Burke

Vanna's sense of frustration is shared by many fellow Cambodian garment workers. The following is an extract from a speech delivered by one such worker, which was broadcast on national Cambodian television with the support of a local campaigning organisation:

Today you will hear the voice of one but the voice represents the story of thousands. Who are the thousands? They are: women, they are workers, they are the poor, they are the victims of an invisible violence – but not less agonizing, sinister and tormenting than the pain and scars of physical abuse.

Where do we come from? We come from provinces throughout Cambodia – we are here because our mothers, fathers, brothers and sisters cannot grow enough to feed us, they cannot earn enough to give us a basic education.

WE ARE THE POOR.

When we migrate to Phnom Penh –

We live in bad conditions – crowded, dirty, unhygienic shacks.

We work in bad conditions – the work is hard – we are berated by our superiors. When times are good for the bosses and they have many orders from abroad, we are forced to work from dawn to night – if we refuse to work overtime we risk dismissal – many of us work on Sundays.

When orders are down, and the bosses do not need us we sit and wait for days or weeks for a chance to earn some money again.

If we are sick they cut our salary.

If we are slow they cut our salary.

If we have to go home they cut our salary.

If we arrive late they cut our salary.

The law sets a minimum salary, but very few of us receive this minimum salary.

We send money home to our families. To do this we eat poorly, and we have no leisure activities because that costs money. Many of us have lived this life for years but we have nothing to show for it – just poor health – weakness, sadness and lethargy.

But we are good enough to make you rich.

But we are good enough to contribute to 90% of Cambodia's exports.

But we are good enough to sustain families throughout the country.

But we are good enough to pay for the education of our brothers.'

This speech highlights the workers' sense of powerlessness and frustration. Just like us, these women have hopes and plans for their future. They have dreams they want to realise, and things they long to achieve. They wish to be able to improve their situation, to build a better life, not just for themselves, but for their children. They are calling out for people to stop, take notice and do what they can to help.

Fellow garment worker in Rokye's factory

NO TALK
ONLY DO YOUR WORK.
কথা নয়,
শুধু কাজ করুন

Sign on factory floor, Bangladesh

Sale sign on shop window, UK

Five

The Fabric of Injustice

'We need a country that asks "why?" not "how much?"'
Anita Roddick, founder of The Body Shop

Our global neighbours in the garment industry, such as Rokye, Vanna and others, have a hard life. It's hard for lots of reasons.

We will explore these in a moment, and uncover the role that companies, and we the consumers, play in it all. There are many issues being faced by the people making our clothes. Here we highlight five of the key ones.

Low Wages

The Clean Clothes Campaign, a European and International network of organisations campaigning to improve workers pay, conditions and rights in the garment industry, report that millions of garment industry workers around the world, including in Eastern Europe and the UK, are earning poverty wages below their country's national minimum wage level. In Mexico, the legal minimum wage for workers is only 25 per cent of what a family of four needs to live on. Workers cannot meet the cost of transport, housing, food and other needs, even working considerable overtime. In community after community, workers can only afford to live in makeshift houses without water or electricity. Nutritious diets for themselves and their children is a luxury their wages will not allow. They work long, productive hours for the world's biggest corporations and still cannot provide the most basic needs for their families.[10]

In China, the wage that is required for a basic standard of living is 60 pence an hour. The standard pay is 16 pence an hour. Workers don't have enough money for nutritious food, education, or access to safe water and sanitation.

Globally, the average garment industry worker can expect to earn an estimated 0.5 per cent of the final selling price of an item. The highest amount they can hope to earn is a mere 4 per cent.[11] The Clean Clothes Campaign recently calculated a price breakdown on an average pair of trainers. It revealed that out of the final selling price of £60, the retailer gets 50 per cent, the brand name 33 per cent, transport costs 5 per cent, the production factory is paid 12 per cent, and out of that the worker gets less than the average amount – a mere 0.4 per cent.

'The supervisors treat us like machines – they shout at us, threaten us.' Martha, garment worker, Guatemala

I recently met a worker from Indonesia, who works in a factory making sports bags for well-known brands in the USA. Her factory produces a bag that will sell for 460,000 rupiahs (£40). To make each bag, there are twenty-one workers in one production line – earning 21,000 rupiahs (£2) per day. Each line needs to make four or five bags per day. The total wages for the entire production line is 441,000 rupiahs – less than the price of one bag!

In El Salvador, women sewing garments for a major sportswear company are employed for eight hours a day and leave with just £2.87. Take away 41 pence for the bus fare, 48 pence for a basic breakfast, 89 pence for a modest lunch (both of which they are forced to buy from the work canteen) and the women are only left with £1.09 for the day. Since even the most basic accommodation (a ten by twelve feet room with a shared sink) sets them back 62 pence per day, they are left with just 47 pence to provide supper for a family of three (which at cheapest would cost 60p). How could it ever stretch to the 68 pence per day per child for childcare? And what about the £4.80 needed for new shoes? What if they get ill?[12] Nearly every nation in Central America is heavily dependent on the garment industry for manufacturing employment. Due to the insufficient wages, malnutrition among women garment workers is greater than among any other group in the region.[13]

Long Hours and Forced Overtime

Workers often have to deal with appalling conditions such as having to work fifteen-hour days, six or seven days a week. In some cases, they are banned from taking a toilet break and have incredibly short lunch breaks, during which they are not allowed to leave the building.

Martha, a garment worker in Guatemala, says, 'I and the other women workers at the plant are very ill-treated. The supervisors treat us like machines – they shout at us, threaten us. Overtime is not voluntary; most women are forced to do overtime and are threatened with lower wages if they don't comply. The wage now is 17.6 pesos an hour (just over £1 a day), which is still below the minimum wage. No one can speak out because they will get sacked. If they are sacked they will go back to even worse poverty.'[14]

When questioned about the issue of overtime, the management of a clothing factory in Mauritius commented: 'Many workers do twelve or fourteen hours, without being offered the choice of refusal. If they won't do it they are "terminated". You can't refuse overtime. If you don't do the overtime you don't have to come back tomorrow.'[15]

Weak Health and Safety Standards

Negligence in the area of health and safety standards continues to threaten the well-being and even the lives of workers around the world. Every year, a shocking 340,000 workers are killed at work, more than a million die from work-related injuries and illnesses, and 160 million more suffer lesser injuries or illnesses.[16]

In 2002 UK shoppers spent over £33 billion on clothes.

There are many health and safety hazards facing workers in the garment factories. These include eye problems and other disabilities caused by poor lighting and long hours. Breathing difficulties are all too common due to dust in the air and workers having no protective masks. Workers who are breathing in dust and threads over long periods of time can be susceptible to lung disease. They often have to sit in the same position for a long time, hence shoulder and back pains can be common. Accidents from broken machinery and dangerous cramped factory floors happen all too often.

Fires have broken out because of unsafe electrics and many people have been killed or seriously injured because of poor fire procedures, or locked exits. In November 2000, fifty-one workers died on the top floor of a four-storey building in Dhaka, the capital of Bangladesh. The women were sewing jumpers to be sold in UK shops. When the women ran to the fire exits they found them locked.[17] In 2002, forty-four workers died in Agra, India when fire consumed their shoe factory. There were no fire precautions, no emergency exits, and no health and safety provision and yet the factory had a current clearance certificate from local labour officials.[18]

No Right to Speak Out

Many workers are not allowed to form or join a trade union, which could offer them advice, support and the opportunity to negotiate their pay and conditions with employers. Until last year, there wasn't a single trade union with a contract in any of Guatemala's 350 garment factories. In Bangladesh, the government banned trade union formation or membership in the Free Trade Zones.[19] Many trade union members and leaders face intimidation, punishment, threats or dismissal if they try to speak out or raise concerns about their situation.

Poor Working Conditions

Zola works in Guatemala City. She stitches 300 collars a day in a factory where it is unbearably hot and the noise is deafening. The workers are locked in, she is not allowed to talk, is punished if she goes to the toilet without permission, and often works fifteen hours a day. Overtime is unpaid.

The workers in her factory say that working conditions are poor. One problem is that workspace is limited: 'People are so cramped that some helpers were actually sitting under the cutting table to do their work. Others were sitting beneath the machines, cutting threads from the finished articles.' There is a lack of ventilation. 'We do not get any air. The factory is very warm.' Meals and mealtimes are insufficient: 'The workers get a piece of bread from the factory before they start working and nothing more during the entire day.' Even toilet facilities are poor: 'There are many problems with the toilets. There is one toilet pass for every fifty-four people. The factory had twelve toilets, of which seven are closed, leaving five toilets for 800 to 900 workers. Workers are searched before using the toilets.'[20]

When we bag a bargain, someone has to pay the price.

Why is this happening? What are the systems of injustice that are oppressing Shima, Rokye, Zola, and others like them?

Fashion Victims

We can read accounts of these 'sweatshops' in developing countries and be appalled. Our first thought might be that the factory managers are to blame. Yet the pressure on the workers to work faster, and for longer hours, starts far from the factory floor. The root of the problem is closer to home. The finger of blame points right back to the source: the companies who place the orders and the shoppers who create them.

In the UK there are over forty large retail chains, 150 medium-sized retail chains and 30,000 independent clothes retailers.[21] This gives us a huge choice as to where we can shop. And shop we certainly do. In 2002, UK shoppers spent over £33 billion on clothes: £18.6 billion was spent on womenswear, £8.8 billion on menswear and over £6 billion on childrenswear.[22]

Yet the big players – the high street chain stores – are increasingly dominating the UK clothes market.

The names of these large companies will be unfamiliar to most of us high street shoppers. They divide up into smaller shops and chains to target different age groups and types of shopper. For example, Arcadia Group owns Top Shop, Top Man, Burton Menswear, Miss Selfridge, Dorothy Perkins, and others.

Bargains

'Bargain: something you can't use
at a price you can't resist.'
Franklin P. Jones

The problems facing the worker on the factory floor actually start with our taste for a bargain. Everyone loves to buy cheap clothes. Shops know this only too well. They know that if they let the price of clothes rise, then bargain hunters like you and I will move next door to find a cheaper price and a better deal. Women's clothing is the most competitive of all and in the past ten years the price of women's clothing has risen by less then one per cent.[23] This relentless downward pressure on clothes prices forces clothing retailers to look for cheaper places to get clothes produced. When we bag a bargain, someone has to pay the price.

To find these cheaper places to produce clothes, many companies move production from country to country, scanning the globe looking for cheaper labour. Low production costs often mean finding factories with the poorest working conditions and lowest wages. This is called the 'race to the bottom' and results in exploitation and oppression for garment workers globally. Why? If companies frequently change where their clothes are produced, it is hard to know which factories are being used at any one time. That makes them hard to inspect. And that makes it hard to check how the factory workers are being treated.

Governments: Home and Away

Governments also have responsibility for the problems facing workers. Bangladesh's government for example, has not raised the minimum wage since 1994 and does not enforce its labour legislation. The problem is that 160 countries are producing textiles, clothing and shoes primarily for export into the markets of only thirty countries, so competition is fierce between them.[24] For the business on the lookout for increased efficiency and decreased costs, outsourcing makes perfect sense. So do Export Processing Zones (EPZs): vast industrial estates created by governments in countries such as Indonesia to attract the wealthy customers with the lure of massive tax breaks and a pliable workforce. Clearly, governments are keen to hang on to their assets and many EPZs have developed a reputation for offering workers no protection of basic rights. Unions are rarely allowed and prying eyes are refused access. More than forty million people work in

EPZs.[25] The number of Export Processing Zones has risen from around eighty in 1975, spread across twenty-five countries, to more than 3,000 in 116 countries in 2002.[26]

It's not only governments in the developing world who need to be taking action to improve workers rights and standards. There is a lot more our government could be doing too. Many UK development and campaigning organisations are calling on the government to introduce corporate responsibility laws, which would mean that large UK companies would be legally required to ensure that they behave in an ethical and socially responsible way. They believe companies should be obliged to publish annual reports explaining their social, environmental and economic impact. Company directors should be legally responsible for taking into account the environmental, social and economic impact of their activities, and affected communities abroad should be able to seek damages in the UK for human rights and environmental abuses committed by UK companies.

Codes Without Conscience

Such campaigners believe that although many clothes companies have made up their own codes of conduct – rules that companies and their suppliers agree to comply with – many of them are just not comprehensive enough. Many codes don't include all of the important International Labour Organisation standards such as guaranteeing a living wage and ensuring that workers can speak up to improve conditions by joining a trade union.

It's true that many also don't tell their customers how these standards are actually put into practice, so, for many there is no way of knowing if they are really enforcing them in the workplace. Many codes are not independently checked and monitored; to ensure that what the stores say is happening on paper is actually happening in practice. Researchers for the Clean Clothes Campaign also found that in some factories the workers didn't even know that the company code of conduct existed or couldn't read them, because they were in English and not the local language. If they are only paper promises, codes will not have an impact.

A growing concern is also that, with much to be gained from appearing ethically-minded, many companies are content with having a code of conduct that puts all the responsibility and cost of improving working conditions onto their supply chain managers, without addressing their own sourcing and purchasing practices. Many companies state in their codes of conduct or PR material that they want the factory conditions to be better and workers rights to be protected. However, it is often their increasingly tight turnaround delivery times and low pricing that actually undermines the very labour standards they claim to uphold. This is a worryingly common problem according to Neil Kearney, General Secretary of the International Textile, Garment and Leather Workers' Federation. He says, 'While these same brand names boast a commitment to labour standards in their codes of conduct, they are at the same time squeezing prices and cutting delivery schedules, further lowering wages and lengthening working hours.' Companies are forcing their supply chain to turn around orders in shorter times, for lower pay so that they can save money and increase profit.

The people who feel the squeeze most are the workers on the factory floor. Merpati stitches clothes for a factory in Indonesia that supplies sportswear companies in the UK. I

James Treasure-Evans/War on Want

Dewi (left) and Merpati (right), at a public meeting

met her when she was flown over to London with a former garment industry worker called Dewi, who now works on behalf of her colleagues as part of a federation of unions representing factory workers' rights.

Dewi knows just how much control the retailers really have over their suppliers. She knows the hypocrisy of corporate giants who claim to value their labour yet who turn a blind eye to the actions of their contractors. She knows all this because, although only 22 years old, she has worked in numerous garment factories in Indonesia over recent years. She has experienced what it is like to work full time – one day off each week if they were not too busy. She was verbally abused when she tried to sit down, having stood for ten hours at a machine. She and Merpati would start work at 7am and finished at 6am the next day when the company had orders to fulfil.

'Eight years working,' says Dewi 'has taught me about the suffering and pain of workers in garment factories. I have a friend who worked in the factory and she cut off her finger on the cutting machine as it was broken and couldn't stop. There was no guard around the machine blade. In another factory, two pregnant workers miscarried in the toilet. They didn't tell the company they were pregnant because they were afraid of losing their jobs and they needed the money. They carried on working.'

Yet Dewi's story does not end with oppression and a downward spiral of poor jobs in worsening factories. After eight years of production work she knew it was time for change. A friend taught her how to defend her rights as a worker, and along with a few others, she formed a union – the first independent union in Indonesia. Within months others were signing up, and one year on, in 1998, there were 22 factories represented. Eventually Dewi's union joined with a number of others and formed the GSBI, a federation of independent unions.

Dewi now works on behalf of colleagues like Merpati, who faces many issues at work.

Merpati explains that if her orders were too big to be met during normal working hours she was forced to work unpaid overtime. She says:

> 'The company sometimes pays overtime but sometimes not. Our wage is 576,000 rupiahs (£36) per month, but the wage needed for workers to meet their basic needs for one person after the union carried out a survey would be

876,000 rupiahs (£54) per month. This wage is not enough to live on to pay for food, accommodation, electricity and medicine.'

For each denim jacket which Merpati stitches, she was paid just 0.4 per cent of the price it would sell for in the UK. Most of the profit will go to the management of the company that owns the retail stores selling the goods on the high street.

Merpati describes the conditions in the factory in which she works.

They are very very bad. There are only eight toilets for 2000 workers. There is no clean water. Many workers are sick. They have stomach and back pain and sometimes fall unconscious or faint. This happens because we are forced by the company to work like the oppressed. The conditions are hot – there is no fan and poor ventilation. There is no air exhaust system, no masks, and no windows – only small vents. The lighting is not good. It is very tiring on my eyes when I'm sewing. There are no eye checks in the company and many have headaches because when you start sewing, you can't look around – only up and down. If you look around at other workers you are punished. We are not permitted to talk. We are called to head office if caught talking.

Many young people in Indonesia like me can't continue their education because of the poor economic situation and that is why they work in factories. It's a bad experience. I was still young when I had to start working in a factory. I had dreams of becoming a teacher but my parents couldn't pay for school fees and so we had to go to the factory.

Merpati is working to make sure her younger brother stays in school.

Workers like Merpati are regularly reminded of the only mantra that counts: Target! Target! Target! If workers miss theirs consistently over four weeks then they are fired. If they meet their target one day, it will be raised the next: 'You can't win. If you don't meet the target you lose out, but if you hit it you lose out too,' says Merpati.

Since beginning to work on behalf of workers like Marpati things have clarified for Dewi. 'I don't have big expectations but just simply want all workers in all countries to know their rights. Knowing our rights as workers is a way to respect our dignity as humans.'

Parallel Universe

Throughout the Bible, God makes it clear that he wants employers to treat their workers with dignity and respect.

In the Old Testament, God set up a social system and structures based on values of justice, mercy and compassion. These systems were radical. They were designed to protect the needs and uphold the rights of the poor and the vulnerable in society. Israel was called to see following their God as a whole life proposition, affecting their treatment of foreigners and the poor, the way they were to trade and carry out general business, and even the political, legal and economic systems and structures they set up.

God set up the Jubilee principle, which was to be celebrated every fifty years. In Leviticus 25 we see how the Jubilee promised life-changing hope, freedom, and a fresh start for people living in poverty. Slaves were to be set free, debts cancelled and land that had been sold was to return to its original owner. God made it clear that neglecting the poor was a sin. Permanent poverty was not allowed in Israel. Leviticus 25:35 says, 'If one of your countrymen becomes poor and is unable to support himself among you, help him as you would an alien or a temporary resident, so that he can continue to live among you.'

God took great care to put in place detailed systems that would protect poor workers who were prone to being exploited. He instructed the Israelites to build a protective wall around the roof of their house so they would not be guilty of bloodshed if someone were to fall (Deut. 22:8). The principle of this specific law can be applied to working conditions today: no one should be expected to work in a dangerous environment. It is the employer's responsibility to ensure that they don't.[27]

God laid down laws to ensure that the poor could not be robbed to line the pockets of the rich. He instructed the employers about their responsibility: 'Do not take advantage of a hired man who is poor and needy, whether he is a brother Israelite or an alien living in one of your towns. Pay him his wages each day before sunset, because he is poor and is counting on it. Otherwise he may cry to the Lord against you, and you will be guilty of sin' (Deut. 24:14–15). 'Do not defraud your neighbour or rob him. Do not hold back the wages of a hired man overnight' (Lev. 19:13). The Old Testament laws about buying and selling land end with a simple statement of universal principle: 'Do not take advantage of each other' (Lev. 25:17).

The theme continues in the New Testament where James paints a vivid and unnervingly familiar picture of a parallel universe – one for the rich and one for the poor. The rich are those who have clothes, silver and gold, own land, and have workers whose wages depend on them. The poor are 'workmen' and 'harvesters' who work on the land owned by the rich and whose livelihoods depend on them. There is a shockingly stark contrast between the realities of life for the two groups. While the workmen have failed to be paid, the rich are hoarding wealth for themselves. While the harvesters who mow the rich people's fields are crying out, the rich are living in luxury, fattening themselves and gathering gold and silver.

James is clearly not happy with the way the rich are living. However, he does not denounce the rich here just for being rich. God's concern is that *they are not doing the good they could be doing* with the wealth and influential position they have. The rich people's lifestyle sins are unnervingly familiar. James confronts them with two key areas of behaviour that, if we are honest, most of us could be accused of:

1. They are more concerned about having nice food and clothing, than meeting the needs of the exploited workers or farmers who produce them.

> Look! The wages you failed to pay the workmen who mowed your fields are crying out against you. The cries of the harvesters have reached the ears of the Lord Almighty (Jas. 5:4).

God makes it clear about the obligation to treat workers properly. Sadly, there have always been people willing to make money at others expense. Jeremiah 22:13 tells us the warning given to Shallum, son of Josiah King of Judah, who was obviously guilty of exploiting his workers in order to improve his own lifestyle: 'Woe to him who builds his palace by unrighteousness, his upper rooms by injustice, making his countrymen work for nothing, not paying them for their labour.'

The similarities between this excessive lifestyle and that of some businessmen are not hard to find. We have all heard the stories of 'fat cat' pay and read about the planes, yachts, houses, jewellery and parties with which those we consider to be truly 'rich' fill their lives. The stark comparison between this lifestyle and the reality of life for workers, who produce the goods that generate such a profit for the people at the top, is just as evident as it was when James was writing.

Merpati is a modern day example of a worker who, as described in Jeremiah, has been made to 'work for nothing'.

People in positions of influence within international companies need to take responsibility for these problems and act quickly to improve conditions for workers like Merpati. But *we* also need to take responsibility. We rarely see the workers in faraway fields and factories, producing the goods we buy. Yet our choices can mean either a decent wage or a pittance for people living in poverty. If we know that there are 'workers' and 'harvesters' today whose cries are reaching the ears of the Almighty, but yet we do nothing to help them or act – then we too have sin on our hands. James 4:17 says, 'whoever sees the good he ought to do and doesn't do it – sins.' The heads of companies are called to pay their employees the wages they deserve, and give them working conditions that are safe and healthy. But what is the good we are called to do? We are called to speak out, to defend the rights of the poor and needy, and to be prayerful. We are called to be compassionate and to 'love our neighbour as ourselves'.

2. Workers were punished when they had done nothing wrong.

'You have condemned and murdered innocent men who were not opposing you (Jas. 5:6).

These verses in James 5 describe how the rich employers took out lawsuits where they wrongfully took away the wages or the land of the poor workers. Left without adequate pay or land to grow food in to sell and eat, the poor workers perished, starved or weakened by poor food, they died of diseases. This was being done according to the law – so that no human judge would be able to hear the complaint of the poor workers. They were kept silent and hidden – out of sight and out of mind. This situation of being wrongfully punished or dismissed is all too common today for workers in the food production and garment industries.

Merpati is one of 170 people who have been dismissed from one garment factory for simply wanting to form a union, to speak out against the unfair pay and conditions under which they work.

The management did not want a union in the factory. They threatened to demote the supervisor and leader of the proposed union and cut the worker's wages if a union was formed. Then, without warning, they dismissed the workers who had put their name to the proposal of a union – all 170 of them, including Merpati.

Some have found new jobs, but most workers haven't. Many, like Merpati are still required to work in the factory until the process of dismissal is complete. They are staying in the hope that their case will be heard and the management's decision will be revoked. They are also in desperate need of their wages that were already behind in payment, but have since been stopped altogether since the dismissal.

Trade has the potential to lift millions of people out of poverty and enable them to fulfil their God-given potential, but instead, profits are being put before people, and trade is reinforcing vulnerability and insecurity. Costs and risks of business are being pushed down the supply chain.

A report from a recent conference held by the Ethical Trading Initiative – a UK based initiative that aims to improve the lives of workers in the global supply chains of the fashion and the food industries – also confirms what we know about how these situations arise in the fashion industry.

Where retailers used to offer four collections of clothes each year, they now opt for a rolling programme of continual new styles, many of which will have taken just six or eight weeks to make the transition from the designer's pad to the cash till. Retailers no longer want to have warehouses filled with stock waiting to be sold. Many stores want to be as slender as their mannequins, unhindered by the bulk of potential failure. Their solution has been the implementation of just in time delivery demands, leaving suppliers with almost one third less time in which to produce the goods. Orders are often smaller and less predictable. Prices have slumped, in some cases by as much as 30 per cent over the last three years.[28] Add all this together and you end up with big smiles at the cash till for us lot, but a serious deterioration in working standards at the other end of the retail chain.

So What Can We Do?

It's really hard for us shoppers to know how our clothes are produced. The clothing industry contains hundreds of thousands of shops and factories worldwide, which makes it nearly impossible to assess the working conditions of every single one. The good news is that there are companies who are putting people before profits. They are trading in a way that benefits, not harms the poor. Trade that not only offers safe and healthy working conditions, but greater quality of life for workers in the developing world.

In Section Three we will take a closer look at schemes that are bringing positive change to people in poverty such as the Clean Clothes Campaign and Ethical Trading Initiative. We will also explore the practical steps that we as consumers can take to ensure our lifestyle choices benefit the poor.

Six

The Hidden Cost of a Cuppa

The fields of the poor may produce abundant crops,
but injustice sweeps it away.
Proverbs 13:23

Durjimoni, tea picker, Bangladesh

Coffee

- We drink thirty-one billion cups of coffee in the UK each year.
- On average, farmers who grow small quantities of coffee beans receive just 1.5 pence from a cappuccino that costs £1.75 in the UK.
- 100 million people around the world depend on coffee for their income.
- Coffee beans may change hands up to 150 times from the bush to the cup.[29]

Tea

- In the UK we each drink an average of 3.5 cups of tea a day.

Chocolate

- The average UK family spends more on chocolate in a year, than a cocoa farmer earns in a year.
- Total UK sales of chocolate were £189 million in 2002.[30]

Tea with Durjimoni

On a visit to a tea plantation in northern Bangladesh, I met Durjimoni. Durjimoni's hair shone in the late afternoon sun as she deftly plucked tea leaves and threw them into the sack on her back. She was smiling at us, as she stood in the middle of a never-ending sea of green tea bushes. The lush tea garden stretched on and on for miles into the distance, as far as the eye could see.

Durjimoni works as a picker in this beautiful, tranquil tea plantation in the Sylhet region. A bright blue sky was overhead, the sun was reflected on the leaves of the bushes and there was the sound of birdsong. At first glance,

'It's difficult to get food.'
(Durjimoni, tea picker)

it seemed like the most idyllic place to work. On taking a closer look, the gentle beauty of the scene contrasted sharply with the harsh reality of the situation.

Durjimoni's job is tedious, repetitive and physically demanding. It consists of plucking ripe leaves from the tea bushes and throwing them over her shoulder into a heavy sack. The weight of the sack is carried on her head, because the bag is suspended from it. Durjimoni's swollen and sore hands show the long-term damage caused by carrying out this repeated action thousands of times every day. Durjimoni started picking tea leaves when she was just 12 years old. That was fifteen years ago.

Durjimoni comes into the plantation early each morning and works for eight hours a day, with one day off each week. After all the years of hard work, she earns a shockingly low weekly salary of 170 taka (£1.67). We asked her if she was happy with her pay. She said, 'It's difficult to get food. It costs 130 taka just to buy food each week – for rice, wheat, dhal, salt and other primary commodities – then there is only 40 taka or less to live off. If I pluck more tea leaves, I get more money. More than 170 taka is good, but if it's less than this I am not happy.'

This plantation is more than just a workplace for Durjimoni. This is where she was born, where she has lived all her life, and where she expects to die. That is no accident. The company intended it to be that way. Durjimoni, like the hundreds of other tea pickers working on the plantation, was born in 'the colony'. The 'colony' is the very aptly named, extremely basic accommodation built for the workers by the tea company. It was clearly purpose-built at minimal cost, without electricity, running water or proper sanitation facilities. Eight or nine people often share a tiny living space, meaning families are forced to share beds or floor blankets. The repeated physical contact over time means that carriers of leprosy spread their disease among family members, with devastating consequences. Leprosy is four times as common among the tea pickers as among the rest of the population in Bangladesh. Air-borne diseases, such as tuberculosis, are also on the increase amongst the tea pickers.

Who would have thought a cuppa for us would cost so much for others?

There is no school, no hospital and no contact with the outside world in the colony. The workers here are hidden people, living hidden lives. They are completely dependent on the company who employs them. Workers live under the threat of losing their home if they were ever to lose their job. So the shell-like housing ensures that families work hard and remain loyal to the company. The workers must ensure that they give no cause for complaint, or they may pay the price by losing their privileges or even their family home.

Before leaving the plantation we asked Durjimoni if we could pray for her. Her eyes brightened and she looked up and asked, 'Are you believers?' When we explained that we were Christians she beamed and said, 'I am a Christian and worship in the nearby Presbyterian Church! My grandfather was a Hindu – and so was my father too – but he became a Christian. He was a leprosy patient and was neglected by the community. A Christian called Dr Cochrane came to the house and brought help and healing in Jesus' name. My father was cured of his leprosy! I became a Christian as a result!'

It is inspiring to see the work that Christians in Bangladesh are doing to show their love in words and action all over the country. Tearfund, a UK evangelical Christian relief and development organisation, is one of the funding partners of the large non-governmental organisation HEED (Health, Education and Economic Development) in Bangladesh. HEED's work in Sylhet's tea plantations teaches workers how to form and run co-operatives, where they can save money, share resources and plan together for the future. They have built slab latrines to improve living conditions in the colony where workers live and have also helped by providing medication. The tea company does not provide a doctor for the plantation workers, only a paramedic who is on hand to provide healthcare for the whole plantation. The workers' low wages will not stretch to paying for proper medication. When Durjimoni and her family are ill, whether it is a very serious illness or not, the only 'treatment' she, like other workers, can afford is in the form of cheap painkiller tablets.

Who would have thought that a cuppa for us could cost so much for others?

At the end of the day, when Durjimoni and the other pickers carry their sacks from the garden to the tea factory, a boy called Sujan is still working hard.

Seven

Comfort Food:
The Uncomfortable Truth

Sujan, tea factory, Bangladesh

'Whoever mistreats the poor insults their Maker, but
whoever is kind to the needy honours God.'
Proverbs 14:31

At first glance, Sujan is just like any other 14-year-old boy.
He likes having a laugh and enjoying himself when he gets
the chance. He loves music, plays football and Ronaldo is

by far his favourite footballer. He would like to be a mechanic when he grows up.

But Sujan is not like any 14-year-old I have ever met. Rather than making great tackles and working up a sweat running around the football pitch, Sujan spends his day making tea boxes and hammering plywood inside a stiflingly hot, noisy factory. He started his full-time job in a tea factory three months before I met him.

Sujan isn't glad to be missing school. He is gutted that his new job means he can no longer study. He says,

> 'I didn't want to leave school, but I had to leave in Class Three because I had no money. I am not happy but what can I do? I need the money. My mum and dad used to pluck the tea leaves, and father made boxes for the tea as well. My mum is sick and now can't work at all, and so I am working in her place. After many years of plucking, Mum's hands are so sore she cannot pluck any more. My family's name is down on the workforce list – we have a work permit, and so if I don't work, our name will be obliterated from the list.'

Sujan's tiny home in the colony is shared between eight people. He has five brothers and sisters, and his family live with the constant threat of the company taking away the work permit and home. In the face of this possibility, they are afraid to complain about the pay and conditions they are forced to endure.

Sujan's shifts are long and his pay low. His first shift starts at 7am and finishes at 3pm. This wouldn't be too bad if his second shift didn't start at 3pm and finish at 11pm. Sujan tells us there is even a third shift – which is optional – starting at 11pm all through the night until 7am. His meagre pay of 150 taka (£1.58 per week) is simply not enough to live on. Even at such a young age, Sujan understands his responsibility to work as hard and earn as much as he can. His situation seems, and is, a world away from yours and mine. But, he, like us, has hopes for the future and dreams he longs to fulfil. Unlike us, however, he knows that he has little chance of realising them.

Sujan no longer expects to become a great footballer, like Ronaldo. He no longer expects to become a mechanic. His dreams have been crushed to fit the size of his reality. Sujan now expects to work in this tea factory for the next fifty-five years or so, until he dies.

Trade: The Bigger Picture

Durjimoni and Sujan's story highlights just some of the issues facing many workers, not just in the tea industry, but also the coffee, cocoa, banana and other food industries around the world. The problems experienced by poor producers will vary according to the product, but the resulting poverty has the same devastating impact. For instance, small-scale farmers who grow coffee and cocoa are generally paid very low prices for their crops. The greatest problem faced by tea producers as we have seen, is that of fair wages and decent working conditions, because most tea is grown on large estates, and workers live and work in large plantations owned by the company.

The poor housing and healthcare, and the lack of clean water and sanitation that is commonly offered to workers living in company owned plantations and land is simply enforcing poverty. Workers are not being treated with dignity and respect. Durjimoni, Sujan and thousands of others like them are being kept in a weak and vulnerable position economically and physically.

Fluctuating prices are a major problem for both workers and farmers. The global price of tea has dropped by nearly a half in real terms since the 1970s.[31] This is causing many smaller businesses to fold, wages to be lowered and extreme poverty to result. In India, for example, up to 65,000 plantation workers have seen their livelihoods destroyed as their estates have been abandoned because low prices

'My mum is sick and now can't work at all, and so I am working in her place.' (Sujan, tea worker, aged 14)

have made them unprofitable. A further 20,000 have not been paid for up to twenty months.[32] Many developing world farmers get paid less per kilo of coffee or cocoa, than it costs to produce it. When commodity prices fall it can have a catastrophic effect on millions of small-scale farmers, forcing many of them into crippling debt, and many to lose their land and their homes. The lives of coffee farmers, banana harvesters, tea pickers and cocoa bean farmers are getting lost in the race for profits and their basic rights are exploited rather than protected.

Fairtrade Foundation Director Harriet Lamb says, 'Low prices may seem great for shoppers, but all too often someone is paying the price – usually the farmers at the end of the supply chain. Producers are frequently faced with the stark choice between facing ruin or selling their product at any price.'

Trade Injustice

According to Caroline Spelman, MP, 'Trade could be the greatest force for poverty reduction in history.' World trade has the potential to lift millions of people out of poverty but the current global trading system is unjust and is forcing millions of people into poverty and causing harm to the environment.

Trade itself is not the problem. The rules and practices that govern it are. They are weighted in favour of rich countries and big businesses and, in effect, against developing countries and the environment. The rules allow big businesses and rich countries to dominate international trade, so much so that poor countries simply can't compete.

Trade could be the greatest force for poverty reduction in history.

All too often, the impact of trading regulations is to exclude poor producers from the income their labour generates.

The World Bank, International Monetary Fund and the governments of rich countries at the World Trade Organisation (including the British government through the European Union) are forcing poor countries to adopt a set of policies, which are known as free trade. Free trade might sound like a good idea – we consider freedom to be a good thing. But in trade, free doesn't necessarily mean fair.

Taken on a global scale, free trade would allow every country to play by the same rules, specialising in producing what they are good at so that everyone benefits. It's a vision shared by the British government, who argue that the continued opening up of markets to free trade could lift 300 million people out of poverty.

But applying the same rules to all countries regardless of their needs means that poor countries lose out. Poor farmers are forced to compete with farmers of rich countries. But they don't have technology, infrastructure or support from their governments.

Dr Robert Aboagye-Mensah from Ghana likens it to a giraffe and an antelope competing for food that is at the top of a tree:'You can make the ground beneath their feet level, but the contest will still not be fair.'To add to the injustice of the situation, rich countries often don't adopt free trade policies themselves. While they press developing countries to open their markets to competition, remove subsidies and allow uncontrolled

Low prices may seem great for shoppers, but often someone is paying the price.

foreign investment they continue to subsidise their own industries! Europe and the USA keep food prices down by subsidising their farmers with £224 billion each year.[33] America's 25,000 cotton farmers receive three times more in subsidies than the entire USAID budget for the whole of Africa's 500 million people.[34] These subsidies allow rich countries to export goods very cheaply onto the markets of developing countries, undercutting local farmers, destroying their livelihoods, and creating a dependence on imports to survive.

Developed countries are also still protecting their own markets through the use of tariff barriers (taxes on imports). When developing countries try to export to rich countries they often face tariffs that may be four times higher than those encountered by rich countries. These taxes mean that it is extremely difficult for producers from developing countries to access markets in rich countries, and in particular, the tariffs often prevent poor countries from processing and adding value to their goods before exporting them.

Although the Fairtrade system helps some farmers and workers in the developing world, for all to benefit, international trade rules must be changed. The statistics speak for themselves. The United Nations estimates that unfair trade rules deny poor countries $700 billion every year – a colossal fourteen times what is currently received in aid and thirty times the amount of debt repayments paid by poor countries. Less than 0.01 per cent of this could save the sight of 30 million people.[35]

For trade to work on behalf of the poor like Sujan and Durjimoni, the governments of the rich and powerful countries need to rewrite the rules of trade.

The Trade Justice Movement is a fast growing group of over fifty organisations, including Tearfund and Oxfam, which has over 9 million members. It is calling for a fundamental change of the unjust rules that govern trade so that trade is made to work for all, with rules deliberately weighted to benefit poor people and the environment – so that poor countries have the opportunity to lift themselves out of poverty. For poor countries to really have the chance to compete, they need to be given a 'leg-up' by their wealthier counterparts, not simply a level playing field. Take Nepal, Zambia and Peru. All have rapidly opened their markets to free trade in recent years, but have had poor records on economic growth and tackling poverty. In contrast, countries in South-East Asia have reduced poverty through successful trade policies that were not necessarily based on free trade principles.

The Trade Justice Movement is calling on the UK government to:

- Fight to ensure that governments, particularly poor countries, can choose the best solutions to end poverty and protect the environment. These will not always be free trade policies.
- End export subsidies that damage the livelihoods of poor communities around the world.
- Make laws that stop big business profiting at the expense of people and the environment.

Ben Stansfield

Fellow worker in Sujan's tea factory

World leaders must rewrite the rules that govern international trade so that they can give special help to the poor. Rich countries have developed by using a variety of trade policies. Poor countries should be allowed at least the same freedom that rich countries have enjoyed to support, protect and strengthen their services, industry and agriculture. Only then will trade become part of the solution instead of a root cause of the problem.

In Section Two we will have a look through the Bible to explore God's concern for justice and his heart for the poor.

In Section Three we will have a look at the organisations, and groups who are taking action to make a difference. We will have a closer look at how we can get involved, the lifestyle habits we can form, and the practical action that we can take to bring change.

Section Two

GOD'S HEART FOR THE NEIGHBOURHOOD

In this section we will take a journey through the Bible to gauge God's response to the situation facing our global neighbours. We'll uncover God's perspective on injustice, poverty and oppression. We will explore the distinctive principles he calls his people to live by. We'll discover the impact our faith should have in every area of our personal lives – how our relationship with him should transform the way we view our culture's values and priorities; how we build relationships with our neighbours; how we do business, view money and possessions, and treat the poor and oppressed. We will examine the counter cultural lifestyle modelled by Jesus and see what it could look like today, for us, in our culture, in our neighbourhood.

Eight

Through the Keyhole

'I know that the Lord secures justice for the poor and
upholds the rights of the needy.'
Psalm 140:12

But I Just Don't See it in the Bible

It was the first comment to me as I ended a seminar on
'God's heart for the poor' at a Christian conference. It had
been the usual thing. About fifty people had turned up,
which wasn't bad for an optional seminar in the middle of
the afternoon. It had been the usual people. You know the
stereotype. Most of them had been drinking Fairtrade
coffee since before it tasted like coffee. They wore badges of
past campaigns about debt reduction, boycotts of
companies and solidarity with far-off causes. They probably
ate a lot of organic brown rice. They came to the seminar
because they were passionate about justice and it was the
one place in the programme that looked like home to them.
They understood their faith in terms of justice and
experienced great pain that their churches thought them a
bit weird. They had prayed, marched, written letters, signed
petitions and were prepared to make sacrifices in order to

stand up for what they believed. They were my kind of people, the sort of people I admire.

There were about five others at the seminar who didn't fit the stereotype. They were intrigued by the title. It was something that they had not considered before, something their churches had not talked about. Maybe it was just a wet afternoon. Steve was one of these. He was about forty and had been going to church for years. He was the first to talk to me as I finished speaking.

'But I just don't see it in the Bible.'

He was talking about whether acting justly and serving the poor was as big a deal as I had been suggesting. He kept saying that there were things he could see in the Bible – such as personal evangelism, worship, personal morality, and so on – that were clearly very important. He could also see that stories like the Good Samaritan meant that we should be kind and hospitable as an outworking of our faith. He was just not sure that serving the poor and seeking global justice was in the same league as these central things. It was not as important.

We don't see the poor in the Bible because we have never looked for them.

I have heard this many times. It is part of our blind spot growing up as Christians in the West. We don't see the poor in the Bible because we have never looked for them. We have been taught that faith is private. That it is about me and my relationship with God. We have been taught that we outwork our faith through the range of personal morality issues: sexual behaviour, personal integrity and acts of kindness and personal witnessing. We have presumed that the Bible is quiet on issues of poverty and justice. This is the problem with parts of the 'pro-life' movement. It is not pro-life enough. God does not just care for unborn children. He also cares for those children after birth, when they are running around a slum or forced to work in a factory.

So, we are going to go on a journey to take a fresh look at some familiar places.

At this point, I have a confession to make. I have a passion for cheesy daytime television shows. A particular show that I can't resist is *Through the Keyhole*, where a panel of guests in the studio are shown behind the closed doors of the home of a mystery celebrity. During this visual tour, the guide highlights certain objects which reveal something about the owner's identity. At the end of the tour, the guide always says, 'Now, who lives in a house like this?'

Usually, it is not too difficult to tell what type of person lives there. The contents of the house give the game away. The 'stuff' that the owner has chosen to put in there, reveals a lot about what type of person they are. Sometimes, surprising aspects of their personality are revealed. It is only by getting the chance to look through the rooms of their house that you begin to understand their true personality and uncover their passions.

I have often found that exploring the Bible is like exploring the rooms of God's heart. The contents are chosen to reveal the passions of his heart. As you take a tour through each book, it is bursting with evidence of his character and concerns. There is evidence of his plan of salvation and his amazing grace, his sovereignty and his desire for our holy living. But there is also evidence of a major aspect of God's character that is often overlooked. One that is mentioned over 800 times throughout the Old and the New Testaments, once every twelve verses, in fact. It recurs so often that if you were to rip out every page that mentioned it, and tried to set the Bible up on its end, it would fall over. This theme is God's heart for the poor and his passion for justice.

From the first time God reveals himself to his chosen people, a slave nation, he identifies himself as a compassionate God who actively intervenes to liberate the poor and oppressed so that his people can worship him. Throughout Leviticus and Deuteronomy God sets up a legal system and structures designed to protect the needs and uphold the rights of the poor and needy. God's passion for justice for the poor resonates through the voices of the prophets Amos and Micah, through whom God warns the people that they will be punished if they don't look after the vulnerable and weak. The fulfilment of this prophecy in the splitting of the Israelite nation is a sober reminder of the importance that God attached to the treatment of the poor.

The contents of God's word reveal the concerns of his heart.

In the Psalms and Proverbs a portrait is painted of a God who not only judges those who fail to act to help the poor, but one who is so moved by love and compassion that he takes action himself to bring hope to those in despair. The psalmist says, 'Who is like you, O LORD? You rescue the poor from those too strong for them, the poor and needy from those who rob them' (Ps. 35:10). In Proverbs we wonder at a God who wants to identify with the poor: 'He who oppresses the poor shows contempt for their Maker' (Prov. 14:31) and 'He who is kind to the poor lends to the LORD' (Prov. 19:17).

In Isaiah we are told of the one who will come to serve not to be served, 'to preach good news to the poor … to bind up the broken-hearted, to proclaim freedom for the captives and release from darkness for prisoners' (Isa. 61:1).

In the Gospels we read about Jesus, the one who personifies justice, love and compassion – the radical servant king. He touches the untouchables, eats with the outsiders, heals the sick, and preaches good news to the poor.

Let's take a tour through these rooms of God's heart, to see what they reveal about his passions, character and concerns, and the challenging truths they uncover about ours.

Nine

Exodus: A story of Justice

The stories of workers such as Rokye, Shima, Sujan and others, are modern, but they are also old. It's hard not to notice the uncanny similarity between their situation today and the injustice facing the Israelite nation in the book of Exodus.

Exodus is one of the most dramatic books of the Bible. There is an evil ruler intent on genocide, a baby hidden in a river who is amazingly saved, a hero, full of human frailty, who battles through to win a great victory, and a powerful, wonderful God who saves his people. It is an exciting, challenging and inspiring story, a story of redemption, but also a story of justice, which is a key theme of the book. In Exodus, God stands against the injustice of Pharaoh's reign and calls his liberated people to a just lifestyle.

At the beginning of Exodus the Israelites are an enslaved and embittered nation. Pharaoh is intent on working them to the ground and destroying them as a people. It is into this context of great injustice that God speaks and reveals himself as the God who sees what is really happening to his people who are the last and the least.

> The LORD said, "I have indeed seen the misery of my people in Egypt. I have heard them crying out because of their slave drivers, and I am concerned about their suffering. So I have come down to rescue them from the hand of the Egyptians and to bring them up out of that land into a good and spacious land, a land flowing with milk and honey … and now the cry of the Israelites has

reached me and I have seen the way the Egyptians are oppressing them. So now go, I am sending you to Pharaoh to send my people the Israelites out of Egypt." (Ex. 3:7–10)

The statements God makes to his people reveal so much about his heart: 'I have seen'; 'I have heard'; 'I am concerned'; 'So I have come down to rescue them.'

This is a God who *sees*. He sees beyond the superficial, right to the heart of the human condition. But he doesn't just see. His seeing floods him with a great compassion that propels him into action. God could easily eliminate the Egyptians and free the Israelites in a moment. But his final statement reveals that God's rescue plan includes the active involvement of ordinary people, just like Moses. *'So now go, I am sending you.'*

Let's look at the situation in Egypt. Pharaoh was unjust. The Israelites had been slaves for many years. Pharaoh and the Egyptians had oppressed them. Children were born as slaves. Sisters and brothers, their fathers and mothers, grandfathers and grandmothers were all slaves. No one knew freedom. Slavery was the norm.

Pharaoh had been carrying out a policy of population control. He distrusted the Hebrews, who were multiplying rapidly and may soon be in a position to threaten his power. The Israelites were oppressed. They were exploited. They were kept in poverty. To the Hebrews, it must have seemed that the situation could never change, because their oppressors had a carefully planned system in place: '[The Egyptians] put slave masters over [the Israelites] to oppress them with forced labour … they made their lives bitter with hard labour in brick and mortar and with all kinds of work in the fields; in all their hard labour the Egyptians used them ruthlessly' (Ex. 1:11–14).

Eventually, Moses asks Pharaoh to let the people go. In anger, Pharaoh decides to force the Hebrews to make more bricks, but without straw, and the injustice increases (cf. Ex. 5).

Food and Clothes: The Modern Day Bricks and Mortar

The nature of injustice in Exodus is strikingly similar to the exploitation, oppression, greed, slavery and enforced poverty in the world around us. The system devised by the Egyptians, of having supervisors who made sure that the slaves worked as fast as possible, is one which is all too common in certain businesses today. In Guatemala, for example, a report from the Clean Clothes Campaign – a European-wide network campaigning for workers rights and better standards in the garment industry – stated that, 'Supervisors hit workers to make them work faster or when workers talk to each other.'

The Egyptians tried to squeeze as much labour and productivity out of the Israelites, while, at the same time, reducing the amount of resources they were given to enable them to do their job. This strategy for maximising profit is common in some modern day business practices. Workers such as Rokye, Shima, Sujan, Vanna and Merpati, are relentlessly expected to increase their output, while working longer hours, using unsafe or inefficient equipment, in unhealthy conditions, and without an adequate wage to live on. These workers produce the modern day 'bricks and mortar' on which our society depends – food and clothing.

The slavery of Moses' day relied on no one speaking out against it. In the same way, the unfair trade of today relies on people like us remaining blind to the evidence. Many thousands of workers have tried to speak out against the long hours, forced overtime, low wages, poor health and safety standards, and the appalling living conditions their salaries force them to endure. Many of them have been fined, punished or sacked for speaking out.

The Exodus story doesn't end with the oppression and exploitation of the Israelites. They escape their captivity.

Exodus is a story of freedom, transformation and hope, where a few ordinary people put extraordinary faith in God and a seemingly impossible situation is transformed.

Moses is called by God to stand up and fight injustice. He is the famous hero of the story, but he is not the only one who fights. There is a group of ordinary people in the Exodus story who are hardly noticed. They are people who are also called by God to take action and speak out against injustice. These unsung heroes are the Hebrew midwives, along with Moses' mother, Jochebed, and his sister, Miriam. They were put in a situation where they had to choose what they would do. Would they fight what was wrong or would they choose their own comfort? Their choices had far-reaching consequences for Moses, and for the whole Israelite nation!

> The King of Egypt said to the Hebrew midwives whose names were Shiphrah and Puah, "When you help the Hebrew women in childbirth, and observe them on the delivery stool, if it is a boy kill him; but if it is a girl, let her live." The midwives, however, feared God and did not do what the King of Egypt had told them to do; they let the boys live. Then the King of Egypt summoned the midwives and asked them, "Why have you done this? Why have you let the boys live?" The midwives answered Pharaoh, "Hebrew women are not like Egyptian women. They are vigorous and give birth before the midwives arrive." So God was kind to the midwives, and the people increased and became even more numerous. And because the midwives feared God, he gave them families of their own.

> Then Pharaoh gave this order to all of his people. "Every boy that is boy must be thrown into the Nile but let every girl live." (Ex. 1:15–22)

The midwives were certainly not in a strong position to take on the powers that be in Egypt. They were both Hebrews and women in a male-dominated society. They were midwives, not members of an underground militia network! Their only weapons were their bare hands. As slaves, they would have been well aware of the consequences of disobeying the orders of the Pharaoh. However, they boldly chose not to co-operate with a system that they believed to be fundamentally unjust and against God's law. The midwives preserve the lives of the babies, and defy the authorities in the process.

These brave women make a series of radical choices. They choose to see their neighbour's problem as *their* problem. They choose to love their neighbour as themselves. To open their eyes to see what is happening, rather than ignoring it in the hope it will go away.

They say no to the orders of the Pharaoh and yes to the orders of God.

They stand up and speak out, not stay down and stay quiet.

They choose to be active, and not passive.

They take responsibility, and don't make excuses.

They are sacrificial, not selfish.

They choose hope over despair.

They commit to do all they can with all that they have.

In so doing, these women choose to trust God and not to doubt.

These choices had huge consequences. God hugely blesses these women's amazing acts of faith. As a result of saying yes to God, and no to the powers of injustice and oppression in Egypt, a chain of events to change society and history were set in motion. For Moses, these brave choices, alongside those of his mother Jochebed and sister Miriam, meant that his life was saved and he was available to be used by God to liberate the Israelite nation. God used their acts of courage to begin his plan to rescue his people from Egypt.

Edmund Burke said: 'All that is necessary for evil to triumph is for good men to do nothing.' When good people, fighting for justice, do something, then situations can be transformed beyond all recognition. If Moses and the midwives had chosen to do nothing, the book of Exodus could have been a very different story.

The midwives and Moses were all ordinary people with extraordinary passion for God, for people and for justice. God used each of these ordinary people's personalities, natural passion and the position he had placed them in to weave his plan together.

Take the midwives, for example. What are midwives passionate about? Babies. Midwives, by definition, are people with a passion to bring babies into the world. Where did God place these midwives with their passion for babies? He put them in a position where they *could see* injustice against the very people group that God had laid on their heart – babies. They were put in a position where the lives of babies were being threatened. As midwives, God put them in the perfect position, with all the skills and knowledge they needed to *take action* to make a difference exactly where it was needed. They were not in a position to tackle all of the injustice that was happening around them such as the slavery, or the hard labour – but they didn't need to be. God had 'purpose built' them for the job of fighting injustice one baby at a time.

At each stage of the Exodus story God puts a person, with a passion, in a position where they can see injustice and can take action to fulfil the purposes of God. Each person has a choice to make. To trust in God and do what they can with what they've got, or decide the task is just too big, do nothing, and leave it up to someone else.

Today, injustice, oppression and poverty are just as rife as they were at the time of the Exodus.

Today, God still loves justice. He still hates injustice. Psalm 11:7 says, 'For the Lord is righteous, he loves justice; upright men will see his face.'

Today, God is still passionate about people – they are made in his image and he wants them to be treated with dignity and respect.

Today, God still wants to use ordinary people like you and I to demonstrate his love to his people and to fight against injustice. His word calls us to see our neighbour's problem as our problem. It calls us not just to see, but to do something: 'Speak up on behalf of those who cannot speak for themselves . . . defend the rights of the poor and the oppressed' (Prov. 31:8–9).

Today, each of us has been created with unique passions and skills. We are each in a position to see particular injustices against particular people with whom our lives intersect.

Who are we in a position to help? Who are we being called to *really see*? What opportunity do we have to take action to love our neighbours?

Today, God is calling us, through his word, to open our eyes, open our mouths and open our hearts to bring change. There is so much each one of us can do through campaigning for change, being consumers with a conscience and simply communicating the issue to our friends and others to stand up against injustice. For Ephesians 2:10 says, 'for we are God's workmanship, created in Christ Jesus to do good works which God prepared in advance for us to do.'

Isaiah 1 tells us what these good works are. We are 'to learn to do good – seek justice, encourage the oppressed. Defend the cause of the fatherless, plead the case of the widow.'

Today we are being called on to challenge injustice – to speak out – to show love, to stand with our global neighbours and say that we care. But how on earth can we do that? By drawing on the personality, passion and unique position that God has given us, to fulfil the purpose for which we were created.

History is full of Christian heroes, such as William Wilberforce, who spent their time loving their neighbour by speaking out for social justice. Many of these people were very privileged and wealthy. Their amazing faith enabled them to choose to reject the lifestyle of their class. Instead, they chose to use their resources to bless the poor, not indulge themselves. They used the unique position that God placed them in to take action for the poor. In doing so, they achieved amazing things for God. Slavery was abolished, prisons were reformed, hospitals and schools for the poor were established, women's rights were recognised, forced prostitution was opposed and child labour was abolished in the UK. These people placed their hope in a big God to change things. We must never underestimate the power of one person, with passion, to work out the purposes of God.

We need to ask God to help us to *really see* what is going on around us. To see whom we are in a position to help. We need to trust God to use us to bring change. Each of us can bring about positive change in the choices we make. There is something practical that all of us can do. See Section Three for information and practical action tips to get you started.

Ten

Isaiah: Seeing is Believing

'Our faith is always personal, but never private.'
Jim Wallis

Life would generally be a lot easier if we could have a
wonderful relationship with God just through worship,
prayer and Bible reading, and if all we had to do were to
join with others regularly to do more of the same. It would
even be easier if all that God was interested in were the
areas of private morality like truth telling, sexual purity and
being kind to those closest to us. All of these things are
vitally important, but they are not enough. The Bible
teaches that we have to love God and love others – the two
themes are inseparably linked throughout its pages. Our
personal relationship with God is important, but so is the
way in which we treat others. It's a lesson the people of
Israel had to learn in Isaiah 58. They had a blind spot that
needed exposing.

Isaiah could be forgiven for feeling somewhat confused
when God told him to warn the people that he was angry
with them: 'Shout it aloud, do not hold back. Raise your
voice like a trumpet. Declare to my people their rebellion
and to the house of Jacob their sins' (Is. 58:1). After all, the
Israelites had, by God's own admission, been seeking him,
praying for guidance and trying to follow him: 'Day after
day they seek me out; they seem eager to know my ways …
They ask God for just decisions and seem eager for God to

come near them' (Is. 58:2). They had even fasted and humbled themselves (Is. 58:3). They were doing everything that they knew, everything that they had been taught, but God seemed to be ignoring them. Why should he be angry with them? Why was he distant? Why wasn't he listening to them? They were seeking God for guidance, blessing and intimacy, the very things that God wanted to give them. Surely, they were the ones with a legitimate complaint against God. So what was going wrong?

No doubt, the Israelites thought they were good people – maybe not the best, not exactly saints, but certainly not the worst. They thought they were faithful in worship and committed to their God. They were also quite wealthy – they had employees (Is. 58:3) and plenty of food and clothes (Is. 58:7). In other words, they were comfortably off. They might not have been as rich as the king, but they were doing all right. They did not have to worry about where the next meal was coming from or what they would wear.

It's amazing what you don't see.

Although the Israelites saw the importance of worship, prayer and fasting, they didn't see that a lot of other things were equally important to God. They thought that God was only interested in a private faith. They thought that going to services was the most important thing, observing religious duty, fasting. They had reduced their faith to a private relationship with God that had little to say about how they lived out their lives with others. They thought that how they treated their employees, how they argued, how they treated the homeless, the hungry and the refugees was somehow outside their experience of God. That was 'theirs' to work out as they saw fit. God's area was the church, the singing and the fasting.

They had a blind spot.

In Isaiah 58 God shows people just how public he wants their faith to be. It is not enough to sing songs – you have to feed the hungry. It is not enough to fast – you have to set the oppressed free. You have to clothe the naked, and provide the asylum seeker with shelter. The people did not know it but it was these things that were blocking their relationship with God. They did not need to fast more, or pray more, or buy a new worship album. They needed to serve, to die to their own comfort and live for others.

God shows them that he is interested in three areas: their personal relationship with him; their private morality and their public lifestyle.

Their Public Lifestyle

Most Western Christians have only really considered the first two of these. We understand that we are to pursue a personal relationship with God. We understand that our private moral choices need to come under the Lordship of Christ. That the Bible teaches us about integrity, generosity and service to those we meet. We have been left in the dark about how to bring the Lordship of Christ into our public lifestyles.

This is the situation of the people in Isaiah 58. God goes through a few areas of public lifestyle that they had not thought about.

Stop exploiting employees

How they treated their employees was vitally important to God. We need to think about that when we are responsible for others. But we all need to think about whom it is that we employ. In Isaiah the workers would come to the farm – they were visible. As we have been seeing our workers are invisible. In a globalized world, our goods come from all over the planet. We cannot see the workers who make our lifestyles possible – but God can and He demands that we end exploitation (Is. 58:3).

Fight oppression

'Is this not the kind of fasting that I have chosen: to loose the chains of injustice and untie the cords of the yoke, to set the oppressed free and untie every yoke? (Is. 58:6) All over the world, there are people who are oppressed – sometimes it is religious persecution, sometimes ethnic or racial oppression, sometimes it is about gender or class. But wherever people are held back from achieving God's dreams for their lives, wherever people are discriminated against, wherever they have a 'yoke' placed on them, that is where God calls his people to act.

'Our faith is always personal, but never private.' Jim Wallis

Act for those in need

'Share your food with the hungry … provide the refugee with shelter … when you see the naked – clothe him' (Is. 58:7). God commands his people to act for those in need. In God's kingdom no one should be without food or clothes or shelter. These are basic essentials for life. In the Western world of obesity, expanding wardrobes and house style programmes, God asks us to remember the ones left out of the party. The ones for whom basic survival is all that they can think about.

God loved his people very much. Despite telling Isaiah to confront them, Isaiah 58 is full of some of the most amazing promises:

'Your light will break forth like the dawn' (v. 8).
'You will be healed' (v. 8).
'You will be righteous' (v. 8).
'You will call and the Lord will answer. You will cry for help and He will say, "Here am I"' (v. 9).
'You will be like a well-watered garden' (v. 11).

These are all the things that the people wanted to hear. This is what they had been longing for, praying for and which they thought God was denying them. God is always offering us promises for a future and a hope. He always wants to come near to us. Nothing can separate us from his love and he spelt out that love by dying for us. Because of his great love, he always comes to us with promises, even when we deserve judgement. He is so gracious that forgiveness and a new start is always available. He never wants to close us down because we have blown it. He wants to meet us in our sin, take us by the hand and lead us out of the mess. He is always seeking to save, to forgive, and to make new. He really is that good.

God does want to give us a dream lifestyle, it is just going to be his dream, not ours.

He was saying to the people that they didn't have to live this lifestyle of justice in their own strength – in fact, they simply couldn't. He reminded them that they were his people, called to be set apart, living distinctive lives. He knew that in trying to live the counter cultural lifestyle he was calling them to, they would often feel weak and lost. So he promised them strength and guidance. He knew that their physical and spiritual resources would quickly dry up, and so he promised refreshment. He knew they would sometimes lose their sense of direction in following his ways, and so he promised to guide them along the journey.

God welcomed them into the eternal kind of life. They just had a blind spot that needed exposing. These public lifestyle issues were not an 'extra' for the keen ones. They weren't things you could think about if you had time. They were affecting these people's relationship with God, stopping his promises being fulfilled.

The same is true for us. As we struggle to maintain our personal relationship with God and his standards of private morality, he calls us to a richer vision. He has come to change the world. He has come to right wrongs, to lift up the oppressed, to transform the life of the destitute. He has come to bring in a new kingdom. He invites us to follow him.

Eleven

Amos: Life with Eyes Wide Shut

'The world is not changed by the mighty shoves of the heroes, but by the tiny pushes of each honest person.'
Helen Keller

It has been said, 'God often calls the unlikely to perform the holy.' Amos was the unlikely candidate God chose to be his mouthpiece to his people, to open their eyes and impart fresh vision. To illuminate their blind spots.

Amos was not the obvious choice for such an appointment. He was nothing special. He was not the son of a prophet or a priest. He was a shepherd. Oh, and he also grew figs. He didn't live in a special place. His home village of Tekoa was an obscure place, deep in the rugged sheep country of Judah, about twelve miles south of Jerusalem.

Amos was a very ordinary shepherd. Ordinary shepherds like him would usually stay in Tekoa, do their job, provide for their family and worship God. In today's world, they would work nine-to-five, be a member of a gym, go to church on Sunday, have 2.5 kids and own a golden retriever.

But God had something else in mind for Amos. God wanted Amos to see something that other people couldn't see, ordinary people living their lives with eyes solely focused on their homes, sheep and family. God wanted to take Amos out of his comfort zone and lead him across the divide into the northern kingdom, from the southern kingdom where he lived. God wanted Amos to see something so that God's people would never be able to see life in the same blinkered way again. He showed him an amazing, extraordinary vision of what was on his heart, a vision of the judgement that would come to the nation of Israel, the nation who had become spiritually short-sighted and desperately needed a spot of laser surgery.

> This is what he showed me: The Lord was standing by a wall that had been built true to plumb, with a plumb line in his hand. And the Lord asked me, "What do you see, Amos?"
>
> "A plumb line," I replied.
>
> Then the Lord said, "Look, I am setting a plumb-line among my people Israel; I will spare them no longer. The high places of Isaac will be destroyed and the sanctuaries of Israel will be ruined; with my sword I will rise against the house of Jeroboam." (Amos 7:7–9)

What was God so concerned about that justified such heavy treatment?

On the surface, Israel looked like it had it all. Many people seemed happy and satisfied. They enjoyed great wealth. Israel was enjoying peace and economic prosperity. King Jeroboam's reign was very prosperous and successful.

On the surface, many people were optimistic. However, the wealthy and powerful people of Samaria, the capital of Israel, had become indifferent towards God. As a result, they had become greedy and unjust. They were cruel and indifferent towards the poor and disadvantaged. With all their luxury and comfort, they had become increasingly self-centred, complacent and unloving towards their less well-off neighbours.

Just like Israel, the climate of our times is one of economic prosperity and success. For some that is. Champagne sales hit a record high in the UK in 2004. UK shoppers spent £33 billion on clothes in 2002.[36] On the catwalks, the red carpets and even just down on the high street, everything seems rosy. But underneath the surface there is evidence of a selfish, materialistic society. The dictionary defines 'materialism' as 'a tendency to prefer material possessions and physical comfort to spiritual values'. Shopping centres have been heralded as the new cathedrals, and packed shelves offering endless choice as the new altars where people come to worship 24/7.

Feeding on a cultural diet of consumerism may seem harmless, but can be spiritually deadly. Consumer culture, with its abundant advertising that acts as a weapon of mass distraction for companies selling their wares, can blind people to the reality of life for those beyond the label. Behaviour and attitudes that God considers sinful, like greed, selfishness and indifference towards our neighbour, have become for us, just like the Israelites, a way of life. For while Jesus is calling us to deny ourselves and pick up our crosses and follow him, consumer culture persuades us not to deny ourselves anything. While Jesus calls us to love our neighbour as we love ourselves, consumer culture entices us to question why we shouldn't put ourselves first. While God says our money is not our own, consumer culture tells us that we deserve to spend it all on ourselves 'because we're worth it'.

Worship With Eyes Wide Shut

On the surface, Israel seemed devoutly religious. In reality, they were blind to what true worship was meant to be. They had lost their intimacy with God. He clearly was not impressed. They were worshipping with their eyes wide shut. While they observed religious rituals and went through all the religious motions, they didn't see how that should impact their public lifestyles. They thought themselves impressively holy as they gave extra tithes, went to places of worship and offered sacrifices. They *didn't see* their need to reflect God's heart of love for the poor.

> "I hate, I despise your religious feasts; I cannot stand your assemblies. Even though you bring me burnt offerings and grain offerings, I will not accept them. Though you bring choice fellowship offerings, I will have no regard for them. Away with the noise of your songs! I will not listen to the music of your harps." (Amos 5:21–24)

So Amos tries to open their eyes.

The big issue is that the rich are only looking out for themselves and are ignoring the needs of their poorer neighbours. He says in Amos 2:6–7 that they have 'denied justice', 'sold the righteous people for silver', and 'sold poor people for a pair of sandals'. They 'trample on the heads of the poor as upon the dust of the ground', preventing the vulnerable from standing up and defending themselves. They have not allowed their poor neighbours to be on an equal playing field with them. They have deliberately kept them vulnerable. God criticises the business practices of his people. It's uncanny how strikingly familiar these business practices are for us today.

Life Revolved Around Making Money

> 'When will the New Moon be over that we may sell grain, and the Sabbath be ended that we may market wheat.' (Amos 8:5)

The rich business people couldn't wait for the festival days and the Sabbath to be over so they could get on with their trading. On the very days when they should have been content to rest in God's presence, and focus on what they could *give* to him and to others, they were restlessly yearning to earn more money. They may have worshipped with their mouths and hands but their minds and hearts were on other things. God's chosen people had lost their distinctiveness. They had forgotten what they should value. Their lifestyle looked the same as everyone else's.

This is a challenge to us. Times haven't changed a great deal since Amos' day have they? Everyone is into retail therapy. Shopping is now a 24/7 business. Sunday? Open for business. Bank holiday? Open for business. Middle of the night? Open for business. We can so easily be sucked into the shopaholic culture – focusing more on what we can get to make ourselves feel better, rather than on the kingdom values we have been called to. How distinctive are we? What are our hearts and minds longing for? Does our worship give us fresh vision to see our cultural values in a radical way? Does our prayer transform the way we think about consumption and materialism? Can anyone see the difference in the way that we live, from the faith that we profess? Have we become so assimilated into our culture that we no longer feel a sense of 'culture shock'?

Money was gained dishonestly

In Amos 8:5, the traders used 'dishonest scales'. This meant that the scales they used to weigh the grain harvested by the farmers would show less than the correct amount. The scales they used to weigh the silver to pay for the grain would show more than the correct amount. So the trader would get more grain for less money.

The problem of dishonest weights and measures, and biased scales is widespread today – just as it was way back in 760 BC, when the book of Amos was written! Many food producers in the developing world have explained this very problem as one of the obstacles facing them as they struggle to work themselves out of poverty. The problem of being cheated out of money faces the farmers on a local and a global level.

At the local level, many farmers, such as Comfort Kumeah, a cocoa farmer from Ghana, are treated unjustly when the person responsible for weighing their coffee beans, cocoa beans, bananas or other goods, cheats them out of money, by doctoring the scales used to weigh their produce.

Comfort is a widow in her early fifties with five children. She faced the problems of cheating before she began to produce for the Fairtrade market. 'We farmers were cheated. People adjusted the scales. We got little money from the purchasing clerks and no bonuses. The farmers' welfare was neglected.'

Comfort Kumeah, cocoa farmer, Ghana

Fairtrade Foundation

On the global level, farmers are being cheated out of getting a fair price for their produce, because of the uneven scales of global trade rules, biased to favour the rich, not the poor.

On every level God's heart for justice is clear throughout the Bible – everyone deserves a fair deal.

> The Lord demands fairness in every business deal; he sets the standard. (Prov. 16:11)

> The Lord hates cheating, but he delights in honesty. (Prov. 11:1)

> The Lord despises double standards; he is not pleased by dishonest scales. (Prov. 20:23)

> And how can I tolerate all your merchants who use dishonest scales and weights? (Mich. 6:11)

Pay for the poor: Down. Profits for the rich: Up

In Amos' day, business people charged inflated prices. They boosted the price. The powerful received profits while the poor received less than they deserved. Boosting the price means that the Israelite traders bought something at a bargain price from the poor who produced it, and then sold it at an expensive price and made a huge profit. This is not the way God intended it to be. When the poor are exploited by being paid little and the powerful rich person receives most of the profit then that doesn't reflect God's passion for fairness.

Boosting the price is something that happens today on our very own high streets, where most of the huge profit margin goes to the retailer. Football kits are sold at a hiked price on the UK high street, even though they are usually produced at a very low cost, in the garment factories of the developing world and Eastern Europe. It is clearly not the person stitching up the kit who takes home the lion's share of the profit.

The rich business people exploited the poor – 'buying the poor with silver and the needy for a pair of sandals' (Amos 8:6). Poor producers were not treated as human beings, but as goods. Traders wouldn't hesitate to sell the poor into slavery if they owed as little as the value of a pair

'The Lord demands fairness in every business deal; he sets the standard.' Proverbs 16:11

of shoes. Today many in the food and garment industries could relate to this in that they are expected to be a highly efficient production unit, with little or no attention being given to their health, safety, comfort or physical and emotional needs.

What would Amos say to Christians today in the light of our consumer culture, the business practices that we often accept as the norm, and the stories of Shima and Rokye? I wonder if he would feel a sense of deja vu. I wonder if he would challenge our complacency, our indifference to the poor. Would he want to reawaken our dormant sense of culture shock? Would he question why our Christian lifestyles are not more distinctive? Why our values and priorities have been so moulded by our society?

'But let justice roll on like a river, righteousness like a never failing stream!' (Amos 5:24). God's perfect justice brings refreshment to those who are thirsty and weak. It brings growth and new life to the dry and barren. It brings healing where there is sickness. It brings cleansing to remove sin's stain. It brings life in all its fullness – a never-ending supply of life-giving nourishment to all who need it.

This is what our neighbours are thirsting for. In the face of our culture's complacency, and indifference towards God and our neighbours, I suspect that Amos would challenge us to stand up and speak out just as he did. I suspect he would remind us – as he did the Israelites – that our faith is something that should transform the way we see and act towards our neighbour, near and far. It should inform the way we choose to spend our time, our money, and our energy, and propel us into a radical style of living which challenges the norm. I think he could easily dust down the cobwebs off his old sermon to the Israelites, as it is just as relevant now as it was then.

Twelve

Jesus on the Street

'Small things have such massive consequences that I am
tempted to think there are no small things.'
Anon.

My husband loves to play, watch, read and talk about rugby,
so when the Six Nations Rugby Championship 2004 began,
I had a gnawing sense of dread that I would be forced to
become housebound for the next few weeks, 'invited' to
watch every single match. I hadn't bargained for the fact
that I would also be expected to watch all of the pre- and
post-match programmes as well!

I was surprised to find, however, that despite my initial
fear and trepidation, I actually enjoyed the whole
experience – and, as I'm from Northern Ireland, became
particularly enthusiastic when Ireland pulled out all the
stops and beat England, at the home of rugby itself – the
fortress of Twickenham. As Ben is English, needless to say
he didn't share my feelings of euphoria. In a vain attempt to
cheer him up after this devastating blow to English rugby
pride, I agreed to watch a documentary that harked back to
the golden era when England had just won the World Cup.

In the documentary, Sir Clive Woodward, the then team
manager, was asked, 'What was the secret to England
becoming world champions?' He replied, 'The reason why
our team have become world champions, is because the
whole team takes the small choices we make off the pitch,

just as seriously as the big decisions we have to make on the pitch.' He believed there was no area of life for his rugby players which should be considered unconnected to the aim of winning the World Cup. He believed that in every single area – what they ate and drank, even where they went on holiday – they needed to be making choices that would help them to move closer to their goal. The extreme extent to which Sir Clive applied this principle was demonstrated when, at one point, Clive turned to a player who arrived ten minutes late to a meeting and said, 'you are not just ten minutes late for this meeting. You have just cost us the World Cup.'

'The team takes the small decisions we make off the pitch, just as seriously as the big decisions we have to make on the pitch.' Sir Clive Woodward

A philosopher once said, 'small things can have such massive consequences, that I am tempted to think *there are no small things.'* The way we live our lives, just as Sir Clive believed for the England rugby team, is impacted by the small choices we make each day, which we often think are not important.

I am a bit of a dreamer. I love to think and plan about the big things I am going to do in the future – which will always start tomorrow, of course. I dream about the big things I'm going to do for God, how I'm going to become more Christ-like in a certain area or how I'm going to serve people in need and be servant-hearted. But then, if, in the middle of these chats about service in the future, Ben asks me for a cup of tea, I often simply can't be bothered to get up and make it for him! I feel tired and lazy, and I'll make a feeble excuse so he will make it himself – and even make one for me while he's at it!

My attitude to the small things, in the ordinary, everyday moments of life are so far removed from the dreams, plans and passions that I have for my life. I think many of us are guilty of this. We are challenged to take small choices seriously. We want to be Christ-like, we want to reflect him in every area, we want to pick up our cross and carry it so we can live like Christ, but we really struggle to apply it in the small, ordinary and unspectacular moments of life. We long to fight injustice, and help the poor, but often our daily decisions as consumers can have a negative, rather than a positive impact on our global neighbours. We fail to see the far-reaching consequences of our seemingly small consumer choices.

Paul Tournier said, 'To live is to choose. It's through the making of successive and resolute choices that man traces out his life.' [37]

Let's look at the seemingly 'ordinary' choices Jesus made in the everyday situations of life and how extraordinary they actually were.

Jesus and the Man Born Blind (John 9)

As Jesus was walking along, he saw a man who was blind from birth. "Teacher," his disciples asked him, "Why was this man born blind? Was it a result of his own sins or those of his parents?"

"It was not because of his sins or his parents' sins," Jesus answered. "He was born blind so that the power of God could be seen in him. All of us must quickly carry out the tasks assigned us by the one who sent me, because there is little time left before the night falls and all work comes to an end. But while I'm still here in the world, I am the light of the world."

Then he spit on the ground, made mud with saliva, and smoothed the mud over the blind man's eyes. He told him, "Go and wash in the pool of Siloam" (Siloam means Sent). So the man went and washed, and came back seeing!
His neighbours and others who knew him as a blind beggar asked each other, "Is this the same man – that beggar?" Some said he was, and others said, "No, but he surely looks like him!"
And the beggar kept saying, "I am the same man!"
They asked, "Who healed you? What happened?"
He told them, "The man they called Jesus made mud and smoothed it over my eyes and told me, 'Go to the pool of Siloam and wash off the mud,' I went and washed, and now I can see!" (Jn. 9:1–11, Living Translation)

When Jesus heard what had happened, he found the man and said, "Do you believe in the Son of Man?"

The man answered, "Who is he, sir, because I would like to."
"You have seen him," Jesus said, "and he is speaking to you!"
"Yes, Lord," the man said, "I believe!" And he worshipped Jesus.
Then Jesus told him, "I have come to judge the world. I have come to give sight to the blind and to show those who think they see that they are blind." (Jn. 9:35–37, Living Translation)

Often, when I read about this encounter with the blind man, I'm solely focused on the amazing fact that Jesus heals him. So much so, that I have failed to notice the other amazing aspects of this encounter. So, let's turn the camera around to look at the moments leading up to that incredible healing. Let's retrace Jesus' steps and have a look at the choices he made on that seemingly ordinary day.

The first words of this passage are, 'as Jesus was walking along'. Jesus is in an ordinary place and an ordinary situation. He is walking along. He's on the move. He is busy. He is surrounded by people. He is in demand; a lot of people want his time and attention. Word is spreading about the kind of work he is doing.

> 'To live is to choose. It's through the making of successive and resolute choices that man traces out his life.' Paul Tournier

Jesus also would have had a lot on his mind at this time. This encounter probably happens not long after he has been accused of blasphemy by the Jewish leaders, when they tried to stone him because he told them that he was around before Abraham. The pressure was beginning to mount. The religious leaders were coming to see him as more and more of a threat.

What does Jesus do in this everyday situation, 'as he walks along'? In this seemingly ordinary day, Jesus makes a series of extraordinary choices.

Jesus chooses to see, not look away

Jesus chooses to notice this blind beggar, this man who is blind from birth. He chooses to see this man who is a nobody, an outcast, a man who has spent his life being ignored and who is considered cursed. When everyone else has turned away from the blind man, Jesus chooses to look at him. When everyone else has perfected a million ways to pretend not to see him, Jesus chooses to see. Jesus chooses to see the blind man in an extraordinary way, not just with the eyes of the head, but with the eyes of the heart. He sees him as someone of value, of worth. Jesus feels such compassion that he can't look away, as everyone else has done.

This man is really an interruption in Jesus' day. But Jesus doesn't choose to see this interruption as something irritating or a hassle. He sees this interruption as a chance to do God's work, an opportunity to be a blessing, and to reach out to someone who feels forgotten and invisible. This ordinary choice has extraordinary consequences.

Jesus chooses to stop, not walk on by

When everyone else chooses to walk past this man, probably in a rush to get on with the rest of their day, Jesus chooses to stop.

He stops because he sees this man as worth stopping for. He stops because he is happy to spend time standing in the place where the isolated days of this man's life have been spent. In the dust, on the street corner, he stops to empathise, to rest beside this man, shoulder to shoulder. He stops because he refuses to see this man the way other people see him, as someone whose life is hopeless.

Jesus has a different agenda. He has an agenda of love and hope. He stops because he wants to free this man from the sense of rejection that he has felt for his whole life. He wants to lift the lid off the box that this society has placed him in. He wants him to be able to fulfil the potential for which God created him.

Jesus chooses to speak out, not stay silent

The third choice that is striking is that Jesus chooses to speak up on behalf of the blind man even though everyone else, including the disciples, has labelled this man as a cursed sinner, whose problems are either his own fault, or that of his parents. He challenges people's perceptions. When the disciples see this man, they are so preoccupied with *why* he is blind, that they don't consider *what* they can do to help.

Jesus challenges this. He says to them, this man is not just a theological problem but a needy person to whom you can reach out with the love of God.

Jesus goes further. He calls the disciples to action, to join him in the work that God sent him into the world to do.

Jesus' choice to speak out for this man, demonstrates to the disciples that he wants *them* to choose to see this man and people like him, the way Jesus

Jesus chooses to see, stop, speak out and act.

sees them. He wants them to choose to stop beside them as he has. He wants them to choose to speak out for people like him, as he has.

Jesus chooses to act, not turn away

When everyone else keeps their distance from this man, Jesus chooses to reach out and touch him. He stoops down into the clay, mixes it with saliva and makes a paste with his fingers which he smoothes over the man's eyes. Jesus stoops down and drags his fingers through the dirt. These are the very fingers that scattered stars into space and moulded the mountains. In this moment the creator of the universe stoops to serve.

What an amazing picture. What a seemingly simple choice to make, but what a huge impact this has on this man's life. He literally goes from darkness to life – both physically and spiritually.

One seemingly ordinary day, as he walks along, Jesus makes four seemingly 'ordinary' choices with extraordinary results. He chooses to see, not look away. He chooses to stop, not walk on by. He chooses to speak out, not stay silent. He chooses to act, not turn away.

This is transformational. This changes everything. Not just because the man is no longer physically blind. Jesus opens up the eyes of his heart as well as giving him back his sight. He sees himself and Jesus in a fresh way too. He realises that he is of value, that he is loved. He realises who Jesus is and kneels down to worship him. The choices Jesus makes turn this man's life around.

Do we realise that the same Jesus who saw this blind beggar, who stopped, who served, who touched him, and who spoke up on his behalf, has done all that for us? It is only if we realise the overwhelming extent of his love for us, what he has freed us from and how he has turned our lives around – that our love for other people will grow. We will begin to see other people differently, the way Jesus sees them. We will notice the people who feel invisible; the ones who are overlooked; the people who nobody talks to; those who are socially awkward; those who don't seem to fit.

God wants to give us fresh vision – to see other people the way he sees them. Maybe you used to feel compassionate about people who are forgotten, overlooked, poor, or oppressed. You used to feel moved when you heard news reports about certain people groups, places, or issues. But over time, you have become busy. Life has taken over. You have had a lot on, and you haven't stopped in a long time, to think about those people, places or issues anymore. Maybe at times you try to convince yourself that even though you aren't doing anything to help bring change to those people, or situations – there surely must be somebody, doing something about it somewhere?

So many of us make excuses like, 'Once I leave university, get a job, get married, or settle down, that's when I'll really start getting active to serve people, but right now there's not much I can do.' But God can use us in the here and now. He often works extraordinary wonders in very ordinary situations.

He calls us to make the choices he would make if he were in our day. Not being so focussed on waiting for the big moment *someday* that we miss out on the opportunities to serve, love and bless *today*.

There are so many people working to make the goods we buy today, who will be feeling the way the blind beggar felt – people all over the developing world, far from the tourist trail, feeling forgotten; people longing for someone to see them, to listen to their voice, to stop for a while, to reach out, and to speak up on their behalf.

I want to tell you about an incredible lady I know who did just that. Her name is Zeny. She worked as a social worker in the capital of the Philippines, Manila. She is an example of someone who saw, stopped and served. Her choices have had an impact and been truly transformational.

Zeny was a very busy lady. She worked in an area of the city which would have had more social problems than most areas in the world. She worked in a very poor area of Manila, close to an absolutely massive rubbish dump called Smokey Mountain, on which a whole community would scavenge for food and goods to sell. Every day hundreds of kids would queue to get onto the dump to try to raise money for their families.

One day Zeny was exceptionally busy at work and she was trying to get past a line of kids queuing to get onto the rubbish dump. As she was walking along, she noticed a little boy crying in the queue. She was running late, she was tempted to ignore the boy and carry on to her appointment. But she felt God telling her not to. So she chose to stop. She went over to the boy and asked him why he was crying. He told her he was crying because he was afraid he wouldn't get onto the rubbish dump that day. The queue was long and moving very slowly. His father was sick and needed medicine. He had to get onto the rubbish dump to find things to sell, so he could give money to his mother to buy medicine for his dad. Zeny decided to forget about hurrying on to the appointment which she was now very late for. She took him by the hand and asked if she could go to see his family.

The boy's name was Eduardo. She took him back to his home and met his family. She made a decision that day that she would commit to supporting his family financially and in prayer. Over the next few years she supported Eduardo through school. He was very bright, and won a scholarship to university where he studied accountancy. As well as supporting them financially, Zeny shared her faith with them. Eduardo became a Christian.

Zeny is an ordinary woman, who, as she was walking along, on an ordinary day, chose to see, chose to stop and chose to ask one little boy a simple question, 'Why are you crying?' Because Zeny chose to serve the boy who started life as a scavenger on the Smokey Mountain rubbish dump, Eduardo's life was literally transformed, both spiritually and physically. Eduardo is now the president of the second largest bank in Manila. He still chooses to live close to where the Smokey Mountain rubbish dump was located. He uses the money he makes to support the work of the churches in the area who are reaching out to poor communities there.

Obeying Jesus' call to 'love the Lord your God with all your heart, all your soul, all your strength, and all your mind' and 'Love your neighbour as yourself' has got to start in the small, everyday, ordinary, unspectacular choices and moments of life.

In Section Three we will take a look at how our everyday lifestyle choices can be making a difference for people in poverty. It is in those decisions that we can choose to serve, not wait to be served. We can choose to speak out for the poor, not stay quiet. We can choose to be sacrificial and not selfish. We can choose to commit to do all we can with what we have, living a radical lifestyle, where we connect God's heart for justice and his passion for the poor with our everyday lifestyle choices.

Thirteen

James: Living Out Loud

'At the end of the twentieth century most of us will not
have to repent of the great evils we have done, but of the
apathy that has prevented us from doing anything at all.'
Martin Luther King

The book of James is about lifestyle. James is passionate
that our lifestyles should proclaim our faith, not just our
words. No other book of the New Testament concentrates
so exclusively on lifestyle questions.

James is also dominated by the person of Jesus. No other
letter of the New Testament has as many references to the
teaching of Jesus per page, although it only mentions Jesus
by name twice. James clearly wants to show his readers that
Jesus' teaching has a lot to say about their daily lifestyles.
James is unnervingly relevant to us today. James' readers
clearly were having problems putting their faith into
practice.

Doing the Word

Do not merely listen to the word, and so deceive
yourselves. Do what it says. (Jas. 1:22)

How can we put our faith into practice? How do we love our neighbour in the dull reality of a Monday morning or in the busyness of a manic weekend? James reminds us of a few home truths about being a true believer. It's not rocket science. It's not quantum physics. It's all about saying yes to God and no to ourselves. It's about 'doing the word' in the ordinary moments and choices of life.

When you drive your car, you can't forget what the Highway Code says. To live the Christian life, you can't walk away from the Bible and forget what you have read. You have to live it out.

Referring to the wise and foolish builders, Jesus says, 'Therefore he who hears these words and puts them into practice is like a wise man who built his house upon the rock … but everyone who hears these words of mine and does not put them into practice is like a foolish man who built his house upon the sand' (Mt. 7:24–27).

James 1: 23–24 says, 'Anyone who listens to the word but does not do what it says is like a man who looks at his face in a mirror and, after looking at himself, goes away and immediately forgets what he looks like.'

Apparently, film star Audrey Hepburn used to have a ritual. When she was out for dinner, after each course she would polish up her knife on her napkin, point it towards her mouth and use it as a mirror to check if she had any unsightly morsels of caviar stuck between her teeth, or soup on her chin.

I remember hearing an interview with an American film star where he was asked by an obviously adoring interviewer, what it felt like to look into the mirror and see such a vision of perfection every single day of his life. He, surprisingly, said that he actually hated mirrors and had a policy of not looking into them too often. He said, 'the more you study yourself in the mirror the more you'll notice things you don't like.'

Many of us apply this philosophy to our Christian lives. Just as the mirror shows us angles and areas of ourselves which we can't usually see, God's word turns the spotlight on areas of our lives which are usually hidden, such as our attitudes, our heart, our values, our priorities.

Studying the Bible, just like looking into a mirror, can make us feel uncomfortable, as it highlights areas of our lives where we should be reflecting God's heart and simply aren't. Sometimes we prefer not to see the areas where change is needed. Maybe it's time to give our hearts an up-close-and-personal inspection, so that we can be honest with God and ourselves about how we are doing when it comes to the area of loving our global neighbour.

Reflecting Reality

> But the man who looks intently into the perfect law that gives freedom, and continues to do this, not forgetting what he has heard, but doing it – he will be blessed in all he does. (Jas. 1:25)

In Peru, I visited a Christian care centre for children who have been sexually abused. The staff at the centre share the love of Jesus with the kids, as well as caring for their physical and emotional needs. They invited us to sit in and observe some of the therapy sessions, which they were running for the children.

The first one was called 'mirror therapy'. The children sat in a circle facing a huge mirror, which covered a wide, high wall. In turn, each of the children was asked to come up to look into the mirror, and describe themselves – their faces, hair and body – to the rest of the group. When we asked the reason for this, it was explained that often children who have been sexually abused over a long period of time have a common tendency to use language, when describing themselves, which should be used to refer to animals, not people. For example, one girl, when asked to describe her hands, used the word which means 'paw', or when referring to her foot used the word that means 'hoof'.

These young children had been subjected to such maltreatment, that their self-esteem was shattered and their self-image was of an animal, rather than a human being. The 'mirror therapy' sessions were designed to build up their self-esteem and help them re-identify themselves as human beings, made in the image of God, unique and special.

It's about doing the word in the ordinary moments and choices of life.

After a time of being taught to look at themselves and re-connect with who they really were, their language began to change. They began to literally see themselves and each other differently. The mirror revealed to them the truth about their identity. It showed them who they were. It showed them that they were not animals, but beautiful human beings. It helped them realise that they were each unique and special, and worthy of love. The mirror was more powerful than simply having a teacher telling each child those truths. They had to be encouraged and free to see it for themselves. This self-discovery from looking into the mirror and remembering what they saw could not be questioned. They had seen the truth for themselves.

This process of self-discovery took time and the children had to repeat the session over and over again, coming back to the mirror to rediscover their identity and be reconciled with themselves and each other. It was not enough to do it once. The kids had such a long history of being treated like animals that they would very quickly forget what they had seen in the mirror. They needed to be reminded of it again for the message to be reinforced.

Realising who they were, and getting to know the loving father God to whom they belonged, had a transforming impact, not just on how the children were able to see themselves, but also on the way they were able to interact with each other.

One girl stopped wetting herself every night in bed as she had done because of fear and anxiety during her first year in the care centre. Another stopped incessantly crying, and frowning, due to deep depression and sadness, and began to smile and take part in activities with enthusiasm and happiness. As the children discovered their own value and worth, their love for themselves gradually was restored and grew, and this had a massive impact on the love and acceptance they had for each other. Their trust in other people, especially adults, was restored, so they were able to build friendships with people who they would usually shy away from in fear.

Looking into the mirror and remembering what they saw freed the children to be who God always intended them to be and, with the truth of Jesus' love for them being communicated on a regular basis, their lives and relationships with others were transformed.

The mirror of truth

Really getting into the Bible and remembering the areas it highlights in our lives can also release us to be the people God intended us to be. Soaking up the amazing truth and promises we find there would free us from the lies which the world of media moguls, glossy magazines and advertising billboards scream at us about what our worth is based on and the things we should value.

Adverts promise us that we deserve a treat 'because I'm worth it', and that once we have got hold of the new shampoo, or pair of jeans, or designer jacket, we will look better, and then feel better and life will be better. We will reflect the happy, glamorous image portrayed in the advert.

The Bible tells us the opposite. It says that the poor deserve to be treated well because they are worth it. It says that it is only when we love others the way we normally love ourselves then we can experience true blessing and refreshment. Then we will reflect, not a manufactured brand image, but the image of the one who made us.

As we become more aware of who we were designed to be and how God intended for us to live, serving others, putting their needs first, then we will see our lifestyle choices in a fundamentally different way.

Choices That Change Lives

What good is it, my brothers, if a man claims to have faith but has no deeds? Can such faith save him? Suppose a brother or sister is without clothes and daily food. If one of you goes and says to him, "Go, I wish you well; keep warm and well fed," but does nothing about his physical needs, what good is it? In the same way, faith by itself, if it is not accompanied by action, is dead.' (Jas. 2:14–26)

In the summer before my final year at university, I went island-hopping in Greece with ten friends from university. On the last day of the holiday, with no money or energy left after a month's backpacking, we spent a morning in the botanical gardens in Athens. As I wandered around the gardens, I came across a domed cage, partly covered by foliage. I peered into it, expecting to see exotic birds, but was extremely surprised to discover ... a very large lion!

The lion was in a pretty bad state. It clearly had no room to walk around properly. The most it could do was pace backwards and forwards in a repeated motion, with a dazed, defeated look in its eyes. It walked forward two steps, reached the side of the cage, and then paced back three steps, when it reached the other side. It did this over and over again. It was heartbreaking to watch.

I felt really upset and angry. How could the authorities in Athens allow the lion do be cooped up in this way? Was no one bothered about it? Surely there must be a better place – a safari park or somewhere where it could roam around as in the wild? I couldn't stop thinking about it as I waited to catch the flight home. Someone really had to do something about it! So, I went to the airport, got on a plane home and completely forgot about it.

Eighteen months later, I was home from university for Christmas. A programme called *Challenge Anneka* was on TV. People wrote to Anneka with a 'challenge', which she was to achieve in twenty-four to forty-eight hours. I almost jumped off the sofa when I realised that the challenge was for Anneka to free a lion, which was being held in a cramped cage in the botanical gardens in Athens! Anneka read out a letter asking her to relocate the lion to a place where it could be free to roam around happily.

An old lady, like me, had visited the gardens and had spotted the lion in the cage. She too had felt angry and upset about it, and wanted something to be done to improve the situation. But unlike me, she saw the lion's problem as her problem. I had talked about it. I got angry about it. But then forgot about it. She took action and did what she could to help.

The show was fantastic. Anneka and her team got permission from the Greek authorities to free and relocate the lion to an amazing safari park for big cats in Kent, England. It was so wonderful to see the lion being able to walk and run free across acres and acres of land, with other lions, which he could get to know. Its whole life was changed because one person did what she could with what she had.

This old lady knew that she couldn't physically free the lion herself, but her seemingly small action set off a chain reaction that changed everything.

She didn't have a set of power tools to break into the cage, but she did have a pen.

She didn't own a safari park, but she did own a stamp.

She didn't have a position of authority, but she did have a heart of compassion.

She didn't know if her actions would make a difference – but she was willing to do what she could with what she had.

It dawned on me that the lion might have been released a full year and a half sooner had I bothered to do something about it. It made me think. How many other situations I had been in a position to do something about – but hadn't?

Who can you relate to most in this situation? The lady who wrote the letter or me? Do you see situations of injustice and feel sad and upset? Do you feel shocked and angry as you read about the situation of workers in the developing world? Do you feel a real sense that it is unfair? Do you strongly believe someone really should do something about it?

For many people who are making the products that end up in our high street stores, they are just as trapped as the lion was in the cage in the botanical gardens in Athens. They are being restricted from living life to the full. Sincere good wishes will not change their situation.

Good intentions and strong emotions are not enough. We need to act. Speaking up, writing a letter, choosing to put people before prices when we shop, and praying for the issue, could make a real difference.

> In the same way, faith by itself, if not accompanied by action, is dead … you foolish man, do you want evidence that faith without deeds is useless? … As the body without the spirit is dead, so faith without deeds is dead. (Jas. 2:17,20,27)

John Stott recounts this interpretation of Matthew 25, by a homeless woman:

> I was hungry and you formed a humanities group to discuss my hunger.
> I was imprisoned and you crept off quietly to your church and prayed for my release.
> I was naked and in your mind you debated the morality of my appearance.
> I was sick and you knelt and thanked God for your health.
> I was homeless and you preached to me of the spiritual shelter of the love of God.
> I was lonely and you left me alone to pray for me.
> You seem so holy, so close to God
> but I am still very hungry – and lonely – and cold. [38]

Are our words backed up with actions?

If Christian living is supposed to be life changing, how many people's lives have been changed because you and I are Christians?

Do our choices change lives?

How many situations has our faith directly contributed to being transformed?

How many broken friendships have been restored?

How many painful situations have been made more bearable?

How many lonely days have been made less lonely?

How many hopeless people have been given some hope?

How many people suffering unfairly have been freed from their situation?

How many hungry people have had their hunger satisfied?

How many sick people have felt better?

How many homeless people have been given shelter?

What has our living faith in a living God done to make things better in our neighbours' lives?

Fourteen

Seeing Through Our Blind Spot

'One way is to accumulate more;
the other is to desire less.'
G.K. Chesterton

It seems so clear. From the Old Testament, the New Testament and the life of Jesus, the message of God comes through loud and clear. The poor matter. They might be exploited workers, refugees, the hungry or the outcast in any society, but, whatever the reason, the last and the least matter to God.

It is amazing that we don't see it.

We have had thousands of talks on holiness, prayer and Christian living. But for most of us growing up in the West we have heard precious little of God's heart for the poor. And when we have, it has been spiritualised to mean the poor in spirit – those who know they have a need of God. We water down the truth. We insulate ourselves from the power of God's word. The air that we breathe has not been giving us all that we need to live for him. We need some fresh oxygen. But how have we come to this place? Where did our blind spot come from? Why have we not seen?

A rich man came to Jesus and asked the usual question about how to get the eternal kind of life. Jesus told him to do what the commandments told him to do. The man was not so easily put off. He had been following the commandments all of his life, doing the best he could, doing everything he had been taught. He knew that this wasn't enough and so he persisted. Jesus looked at him and said that there was one thing he lacked. He told him to go and sell everything that he had and give it to the poor and to start following him. The man went away sad because he had great wealth.

Jesus then shocked everyone by saying that it was really hard for a rich man to enter the kingdom of heaven, harder than for a camel to go through the eye of a needle.

I have heard lots of talks on this passage and almost all of them spend their time trying to explain that Jesus did not mean what he said. They say that you don't have to sell all your possessions, just be willing to do so. That Jesus was talking figuratively. It was an exaggeration to make the point. He didn't mean it literally or if he did, he only meant it for this one person. We obviously find this a very scary passage, especially if Jesus meant it.

But what if he did mean it?

I find this one of the most challenging of Jesus' conversations. It goes against everything that I have been taught. We in the West pursue a dream. In many ways, it is a good dream. It is a dream of comfort and security and happiness and the ability to realise our potential. To follow our dream we study hard to get a good job and then we work hard to get a better salary, and so on. In pursuit of this dream, we work long hours, make great sacrifices and show enormous dedication. There is so much of the dream that is good. But it is not the dream of God's kingdom. It is not God's dream.

I think that this is what so shocked the people listening to Jesus' conversation with the rich young ruler. This young man was living the dream. He had power, money and respect. He was moral and spiritual as well. He would have been a pillar of most of our churches. He was a good man. But he was following the wrong dream. Like the others that we have met, he had a blind spot. God wanted more than his tithe and his religion, he wanted to captivate him with a new dream – the dream of the kingdom.

Jesus explains his mission in Luke 4: 'The spirit of the Lord is on me, because he has anointed me to preach good news to the poor. He has sent me to proclaim freedom for the prisoners and recovery of sight for the blind, to release the oppressed, to proclaim the year of the Lords favour' (Lk. 4:18-19).

Jesus was in the synagogue. He had caused quite a stir by healing a few people during the preceding week and now all eyes were turned to him. He picked up the scroll and read out the passage. It was from Isaiah, but they are words that are repeated throughout the Old Testament. They are the dream of the Messiah and his reign.

All of the prophets looked forward to the day when the Messiah would come and begin a new way of living. A day that would see people put right with God and put right with each other. One that enabled people to be at peace with God and live in peace with each other and that empowered them to live a life of service to God and service to each other. It would be a new way of living that was practical and concerned with the every day things. Of course, it would include worship, forgiveness and personal salvation. It would also include healing and acts of God's power over the things that bind people up. But it would transform the way that people lived. This new way of living would certainly include things like sexual morality, but it also included morality about owning property, the use of wealth and the way that the last and the least should be treated.

The phrase 'year of the Lord's favour' or Year of Jubilee was not just a nice form of words but also a programme of radical change that was first talked about in Leviticus 25. During this special year, debts were cancelled, slaves set free and property returned to the original owner.

In the Old Testament, land was everything. It was where you lived but also where you grew crops or kept animals. It was your livelihood. As time passed some families would do well and some would do badly. Some families would have to sell their land making them dependent on others. The Year of Jubilee, which happened every fifty years, returned all the land to the families who first owned it. In this way no family could grow richer and richer over the generations and no family poorer and poorer. Every fifty years things were put right – economically, socially and relationally. This is part of the dream of God's kingdom.

Mary, the mother of Jesus sings about this dream at the beginning of Luke's Gospel: 'My soul glorifies the Lord and my spirit rejoices in God my Saviour ... He has brought down rulers from their thrones but has lifted up the humble. He has filled the hungry with good things but has sent the rich away empty' (Lk. 1:46,52,53).

The little baby that she was carrying – God made flesh – would introduce a new way of living where the humble and the hungry would be the winners and the rich and the powerful sent away.

So, Jesus introduced a powerful dream of a new way of living, but he was not an idle dreamer. He lived it out. He lived his dream when he gave the tax collectors and the prostitutes a new chance. He followed his dream when he confronted religious hypocrites and powerful rulers. He demonstrated his dream when he healed the sick and delivered people from oppression. He fulfilled the dream of the hungry when he fed the 5000. He realised the dreams and hopes of the powerless when he confronted the exploitative trade at the temple by challenging the moneylenders. Whenever Jesus met someone – be it the woman caught in adultery, Nicodemus, the woman at the well, or the fisherman disciples – his dream confronted and challenged them, and opened up a new way of living.

It was a powerful dream and he lived it to the very end. Everything that could have destroyed his dream came against him. Everything that would have revealed his dream as just so much wishful thinking was thrown at Jesus, and he stayed true. He was lied about, but kept on loving. Abused and assaulted, but kept on loving. He was betrayed and let down by his best friends, but kept on loving. He was falsely accused, but kept on loving. He was despised, rejected and humiliated, but kept on loving. He knew what it was to be bullied and excluded and put down, to have his words wilfully misinterpreted and used against him, but he kept on loving. He knew what it was to be utterly alone, but he kept on loving. On the cross he suffered all that could possibly come against a human being. He was 'filled up' with sin. He felt and experienced it all, but said, 'Father forgive them'. Love won the day. Jesus had stayed true to the dream of the kingdom, which burst into reality through his death into resurrection.

Jesus' dream is powerful enough for all who dared to follow. It is a dream that we can trust because it has been tested to the absolute limit. It is a dream that we can live for because Jesus died to make it true and real. It is a dream that will one day be fully realised because Christ is risen and one day all things will come under his rule.

This was not the dream that the rich young ruler was following.

We always concentrate on what Jesus asked the rich man to give up. It scares us so much that we miss what Jesus offered him. In Luke 18:22 Jesus says to him, 'You still lack one thing. Sell everything you have and give to the poor, and then you will have treasure in heaven. Then, come follow me.'

Jesus offered the man his heart's desire – the eternal kind of life, treasure in heaven that would never spoil. He offered him the chance to spend his life on the things that were eternally important, to live the dream of God. Jesus also offered the man friendship. He invited him to become one of his followers. It is the same form of words used to call the disciples. Jesus was asking this man to become one of his close friends and work with him for this new kingdom. Jesus offered him everything he wanted. The man turned it down because the 'stuff' was too important to him. The clothes, houses, food and lifestyle meant too much.

God wanted more than his tithe and his religion, he wanted to captivate him with a new dream.

He wanted the eternal kind of life; he wanted to live God's kingdom dream, but not that much. He went away sad.

I find this one of the most challenging of Jesus' conversations. I am that man. I have a computer. My food is kept in a fridge. I have more clothes than I can wear and I live in a house. In global terms I am rich. And like the man in the story I often feel dissatisfied. My prayer life seems stale, the Bible dry. In a desperate attempt to get back on the rails I pray more, start a new Bible reading programme and participate in church more fully.

All of these are important things, but maybe none of them are the 'one thing' I lack. Maybe my problem is that my heart is divided. All the comforts, toys and 'stuff' that are on offer are more important to me. Sure I give, but the majority of my income remains being spent on me, and my expectations for house, holidays and fun increase year after year. Maybe the antidote – the path to the eternal kind of life – lies in Jesus' words to this rich man. Maybe I need to decide which dream I am following.

Sadly, our Christianity has often not challenged the Western dream but affirmed it. Relationship with God and participation in his family are the 'icing on the cake' of our comfortable lives. We want both dreams – the Western one and the kingdom one. The problem is that we have to choose. Jesus said that you cannot have two masters. You cannot serve both God and money. Like the rich man in the story, you have to choose.

The man and the others listening were shocked because no one had thought that having too many possessions could separate you from God. Neither do we.

We live in an age of stealth warfare. Much is made of aeroplanes that have the ability to evade radar, arrive at their destination undetected and then deliver the deadly cargo of bombs. The people on the ground have no clue as to what is going to happen. One minute everything is fine, the next it is chaos. The plans for their destruction had been made hours or days before, but they had no idea.

It is similar to the old story of the frog being slowly boiled to death in a pan. If you tried to put the frog in to hot water he would jump out immediately. If you put him into cold water and then slowly heat it up, the frog will swim around happily until he is dead.

That is what is happening to us. We are under stealth attack. The water is slowly heating and we are slowly dying.

Our spiritual radar can only spot the things we have been trained to look for – backsliding, sexual sin, anger and bitterness. But we have been blind to the issues of justice and poverty. We don't even know that we are sinning.

I once listened to an impassioned young mother determined to protect her child from the 'dangers' of Harry

Potter. She wanted nothing to do with magic or witchcraft coming near her home. She wanted to protect her child from being scared or being intrigued. If a 'fun' story like Harry Potter made magic normal then maybe her child would develop an unhealthy interest in the occult. Maybe it would be an opportunity for the enemy to harm them as a family.

I have nothing but respect for the mother's desire to seriously consider what was beneficial or harmful to her child. I have nothing to say about the rights or wrongs of Harry Potter. My problem was we were talking in her living room which was full of expensive, electrical toys, board games and books. In the garden, there was a trampoline and a whole set of buggies and tricycles, all for a five year old. The mother and her son were dressed beautifully in designer gear. There were labels everywhere. They had two cars and two or three holidays a year (one was always abroad). When they visited other friends in their church most of them lived similar lifestyles – or wanted to. Strangely, they did not consider themselves that well-off as a family.

We want both dreams – the western dream and the kingdom one. The problem is we have to choose.

The mother who was so concerned about the negative influence of Harry Potter had not for one moment considered that they might be damaging their child by their pursuit of the Western dream. She had not considered that their exposure to consumerism and materialism might harm their ability to relate to God.

Maybe you identified with the mother and her lifestyle and are quite shocked that I am questioning it. Maybe even a little defensive. It is probably how the rich young ruler felt. Jesus exposed an area of discipleship that he had not considered. He had been trying to do everything right but somehow had been waylaid by money and possessions. The water that had seemed so lovely had just become hot under Jesus' words and he was dying. Money and possessions had been a stealth attack on his spirituality and he was devastated.

That attack has been largely successful with Western Christians. We focus on the private morality issues (and sadly don't always do that well with them) and miss the public lifestyle issues that God calls us to. We know that adultery is wrong. We don't know that consumerism is wrong. We are sensitive to the occult but not to our ever increasing desire for more stuff. And so we follow our dream. We work harder than ever. Borrow more than ever. Spend more than ever. And we don't have that much time or energy for God's dream. We are committed to our lifestyles. We are comfortable and don't wish to be disturbed. But we have to choose. You really cannot follow two masters.

Fifteen

Switching On The Light

'Live simply so that others may simply live.'
Tony Campolo

Matthew 6 is one of the most powerful presentations of Jesus' teaching for our times. Here, Jesus addresses our blind spot and calls us to a better way.

The chapter starts with Jesus calling people to integrity in the 'secret place'. He commands them not to be like the hypocrites who do all their good works and religious activity in public so that people can see and admire them. He talks about our Father who sees what we do in secret and in that secret place rewards us. For Jesus, it is who we are in this secret place that matters more than who we are in public. Someone has defined character as who we are when no one is looking. It is the thoughts in my head, the actions that are done in private that are the measure of my maturity and spiritual development. We all fill our secret places with lots of things – some good, some bad. One of the ways of checking our spiritual health is to notice the things that we daydream about. What goes through our minds when our brain is on 'idle'? It is this secret place that defines our discipleship. In Matthew 6, Jesus gives us three great disciplines to fill our secret place – prayer, fasting and giving. These great disciplines directly confront the three great temptations of independence, consumerism and love of money. These disciplines are to be the rhythm of the true

Christian's life and the rest of the chapter shows how to put them into practice.

Independent Living

One of the greatest temptations is for us to be independent of God, to live in our own strength, to come up with our own solutions and make our own decisions. When the devil tempted Jesus in the wilderness he took him to a high place and showed him all the kingdoms of the world. 'Bow down and worship me,' the devil said, 'and all of these will be yours' (Mt. 4:9). This is the temptation to independence from God. Jesus' destiny was to rule over all the earth, but God's plan for this destiny involved service and sacrifice, including the cross. The devil was tempting Jesus with an easier option. He was tempting him to make up his own path, ignoring the Father. Jesus' reply was, 'It is written, "Worship the Lord your God, and serve him only"' (Mt. 4:10). Choosing an independent way eventually means playing into the hands of the enemy. The antidote is personal prayer and worship. For this temptation Jesus invites us into prayerful intimacy with the Father. In Matthew 6:9–13 he teaches us to pray and gives us a model prayer. We are not just to pray for show or on special occasions but to develop a life of submissive intimacy with the Father in the secret place where we align ourselves to his will and lay down our personal kingdoms to seek his kingdom and glory. And the Father who sees what is done in secret will reward us.

This is the starting point. A relationship with God that is real and honest and vibrant is the foundation for everything else. This is how we connect to the great dream of God's kingdom. When the disciples heard Jesus' words to the rich young ruler about how hard it is for the rich to be saved they were astonished and said 'Who then can be saved?' Jesus answered them, 'With man this is impossible but with God all things are possible' (Mark 10). If we are going to follow Jesus' dream we will need to connect with God's power. If we are going to look the great forces of our age in the face and choose a better way then we will need God because we do not have the strength in ourselves. Remember that Jesus offered the rich young ruler friendship and companionship and in that context asked him to give up his possessions. It is only by pursuing friendship and companionship with God that we will be able to follow his dream of justice and compassion.

Love of Money

Do not store up for yourselves treasures on earth, where moth and rust destroy, and where thieves break in and steal. But store up for yourselves treasures in heaven, where moth and rust do not destroy, and where thieves do not break in and steal. For where your treasure is there your heart will be also. The eye is the lamp of the body. If your eyes are good, your whole body will be full of light. But if your eyes are bad, your whole body will be full of darkness. If then the light within you is darkness, how great is that darkness! No one can serve two masters. Either he will hate the one and love the other, or he will be devoted to the one and despise the other. You cannot serve both God and money. (Mt. 6:19–24)

Jesus presents us with a clear choice – two different ways of living; two definitions of treasure; two ways of seeing; two masters to serve. There is no middle option, no comfortable fudge – just a choice.

On the one hand, there is the pursuit of treasure on earth – a life dominated by acquiring things and experiences and a lifestyle. Jesus calls this serving money. On the other hand, there is the pursuit of treasure in heaven – a life dominated by acquiring an ever-deeper relationship with God and obedience to his will. It is a choice.

Jesus talked a lot about money. Sometimes it was in big talks, like this verse from the Sermon on the Mount, and sometimes it was one-to-one, like his conversation with the rich young ruler. Whenever he talked and to whomever he talked, Jesus was really clear – money is dangerous. We have misunderstood this truth and, consequently, have, like the rich young ruler, often gone away sad.

We like to think of money as neutral, as something that we can use for either good or bad. It is like water. A bit to quench thirst is essential. A flood that brings drowning is dangerous. The question is not how much you have but what you do with it and what your attitude is to it. Jesus seems to say that there is more to money than this – that somehow it has the power to steal our hearts away; that humans often end up loving money and the things it can buy more than loving God and the things he wants to do. This is why Jesus talked in terms of having to choose.

We know that God created everything and that it was good. We know that God is the great provider. All through the Old Testament we see God providing for his people and blessing them with material things. God loved feasts and celebrations. There is nothing drab or grudging about God. He is extravagant and exuberant in all that he does and we are to enjoy all the things he has made.

We also know that all through the Bible and church history men and women who have been serious about seeking God have had to deal with the love of money in their lives. The very material things that should be a blessing have the power to steal our hearts away from God. The gifts from God to humanity have the power to become more important to us than the Giver himself and we end up worshipping the created rather than the creator.

When this happens, we lose the ability to see clearly. This is why we have our blind spot about the Bible's clear teaching on justice, poverty and wealth. Jesus said that when our eyes are bad – looking in the wrong direction – then we would be full of darkness. We will not be *Character is who we are when no one is looking.* able to see. This is why so many people are unaware of the things that Jesus said about money. This is why we have defined discipleship to a narrow range of personal morality issues and forgotten that God is interested in so many other things as well. We have lived for the Western dream of comfort and security and opportunity for so long and so determinedly that we have lost the ability to see. We have our treasure and it is on earth and our hearts have been captivated and captured by it.

Sadly, treasure on earth is not very secure. The things we buy, the experiences and lifestyle that we pursue, break and fade and are sometimes damaged and stolen by others (Mt. 6:19). In any event, they will not last forever. The kingdom dream of Jesus is coming to make all things new. There will be a new heaven and a new earth. There is going to be a day of reckoning when things are put right. The treasure that will stand on that day is not savings accounts and cars and houses and clothes and 'stuff'. The treasure for that day is a consistent, intimate friendship with God. It is acts of obedience to his will. It is acts of service and sacrifice to others – especially secret, hidden acts. That is the treasure that will last forever. That is what Jesus tells us to be captivated with. That is where our hearts should be.

This is what Paul meant when he wrote, 'I have learned to be content whatever the circumstances. I know what it is to be in need, and I know what it is to have plenty. I have learned the secret of being content in any and every situation, whether well fed or hungry, whether living in plenty or in want. I can do everything through him who gives me strength' (Phil. 4:11–13). Paul's heart was with his treasure, firmly stored in heaven with the Father. The stuff on earth was nice and he enjoyed it when it was available but he was not seeking it. His purpose was different. He was focused on the eternal kind of life, on the kingdom dream. He neither despised material things nor required a certain level of lifestyle in order to function properly. He had learned to be content whatever his lifestyle because his heart was not captivated by those things.

The answer is to give things away. The second great discipline that Jesus calls us to is generous, selfless giving. For many of us, our 'secret place' – the thoughts and desires of our hearts – is filled with the love of money. We think about shopping and what we will buy. We collect magazines about houses or cars or gadgets that fuel our desire to acquire some new stuff and we spend our days wistfully thinking about the things we would buy, the places we would go, the things we would do if only we earned just a little bit more. Jesus calls us to a better way. He asks us to fill our secret place with giving. To spend our time working out how we can bless and serve others. To be absorbed by thinking about how we can encourage someone else, how we can make their day better.

The only way to be free from the love of money is to give it away. It is a change of focus from 'what can I get?' to 'what can I give?' When we voluntarily give up something, it stops having power over us. That is why Jesus told the rich young ruler to sell everything and give it to the poor. That was the path to freedom for this man. All the 'stuff' was controlling him. His treasure was on earth and he could no longer see. Giving it away was the only thing that could free him.

Jesus faced this temptation in the wilderness. He had been fasting and was hungry. The devil came to him and suggested that he should satisfy his hunger by turning stones into bread and eating it. This has always struck me as the most reasonable of Jesus' temptations. God has provided food for our bodies. There is no sin in eating. Yet, Jesus said no, and then, 'It is written, "Man shall not live on bread alone, but on

When we voluntarily give up something, it stops having power over us.

every word that comes from the mouth of God"' (Mt. 4:4). The sin was not the food but the priority. Jesus was saying that as important as food is, as important as our material needs are, there is something even more important – our relationship with God and commitment to his purposes. The temptation here was for Jesus to use his power to provide for his own needs and comfort. It was a temptation to limit God to one area of his life – he had just been fasting and praying – and look after himself the rest of the time. The question was whether Jesus would place his personal comfort above his relationship with God.

This is our temptation as well. Will we use all the abilities, skills and opportunities that God has given us for our comfort or for his purposes? What do we need to live on? Is it a certain standard of living, designer clothes, a car?

Or do we die if we are not hearing words from the Father? This is the choice. Jesus invites us to align ourselves with God and his kingdom dream. Like he did with the rich young ruler, Jesus offers us intimacy and relationship. Like the rich young ruler, we need to decide where our treasure – and our hearts – is kept.

> We brought nothing into the world and we can take nothing out of it. But if we have food and clothing, we will be content with that. People who want to get rich fall into temptation and a trap and into many foolish and harmful desires that plunge men into ruin and destruction. For the love of money is a root of all kinds of evil. Some people eager for money have wandered from the faith and pierced themselves with many griefs. (1 Tim. 6:7–10)

Consuming Passions

> Do not worry, saying, "What shall we eat?" or "What shall we drink?" or "What shall we wear?" For the pagans run after all these things and your heavenly Father knows that you need them. But seek first his Kingdom and his righteousness, and all these things will be given to you as well. (Mt. 6:31–33)

The last section of Matthew 6 gets to the heart of the Western dream. Jesus addresses the energy and passion and worry that people put into material things. Many of us get our identity from the things we buy. This is the basis of the power of advertising. If I buy those trainers and wear that aftershave, then I will be that kind of person and those kinds of people will like me. If I wear these sorts of clothes, others will view me as being that sort of person. If I live in this kind of house, drive this kind of car and have this kind of lifestyle, then I will be this kind of person. And so we worry, we work and we devote ourselves to a merry–go-round of consuming, so that we can maintain our identities, project the right image and be the kind of people that we want to be. And Jesus speaks one word into this experience.

> *'Live simply so that others may simply live.'*
> Tony Campolo

Stop!

Stop the merry-go-round. Stop the constant chasing after things, experiences and 'stuff'. Stop worrying about it all. Stop devoting mental and emotional energy to what you have and have not got; what you can and cannot afford; what you will or will not be able to do.

Stop!

Stop trying to build an identity by purchasing external things. Stop trying to hide who you really are behind a façade of clothes, houses and lifestyle. Stop thinking that what is on the outside matters more than what happens in the secret place. Stop believing the adverts.

Stop!

Stop buying stuff. Most of us have more clothes than we can wear, more food than we can eat, more entertainment than we can enjoy. These are not the things that we need. We are craving relationship, community, intimacy and meaning. These are not found in the glossy magazines, the slick adverts and the fantasy lifestyles of the rich and famous. They are found in intimate closeness to our Father, in seeking his kingdom and way of living (righteousness), in serving others quietly and sacrificially.

We have got to the point where the act of buying something is more pleasurable than using the thing that we buy. We enjoy shopping. It is our number one leisure pastime, whether it is in the high street, the malls, the catalogues or on ebay. We love to shop. It is our celebration when things go well and our therapy when we are low. We have more stuff than we could possibly use and yet we buy more. And Jesus asks us to stop – not because he is a killjoy but because he knows that it is killing us. He loves us so much that he knows the things we have need of (Mt. 6: 32) and what we need most of all is to connect with God and his kingdom dream. Everything else is just stuff to help us. We have swapped what is really important for the toys and bangles of the shopping mall – and then wonder why our faith does not seem vibrant, powerful and real.

It gets worse. Not only do we dedicate ourselves to consuming more, we think that God exists to give us the lifestyles that we dream of. That God exists to enable us to live the Western dream. This is why there are so many crises of faith when life does not work out. We didn't get the job or the university place or the boy or the girl or whatever and we blame God. As if God's job was to give us what we wanted. We end up using God to get our way and when it turns out that he has plans of his own we turn our backs on him in a huff and decide that he is not real. We forget that Jesus called us to follow him where he was going and not the other way round.

Jesus faced this temptation:

The devil took him to the Holy City and had him stand on the highest point of the temple. "If you are the Son of God," he said, "throw yourself down for it is written 'He

will command his angels concerning you, and they will lift
you up in their hands, so that you will not strike your foot
against a stone.'" Jesus answered him, "It is also written:
Do not put the Lord your God to the test." (Mt. 4:5–7)

Jesus is going to be lifted up and glorified before all
peoples. That is his destiny. The devil offers Jesus another
shortcut, by suggesting that Jesus puts on a show, i.e. that
he goes to the top of the temple and throws himself off.
God had, after all, promised to care for him. God would
protect Jesus and everyone would see how great he was
and listen to him. And Jesus says stop.

The temptation was to use God to get his own way. It was a
perversion of God's promise to him. It was taking the promise
of God and demanding that God fulfilled it in a particular way.
It was using God, and Jesus said no. God has promised us
that he knows what we need. So much of Western Christianity
has been about demanding that God fulfil our consuming
passions in the ways we choose and when we choose. We end
up putting God to the test as to whether he will deliver our
lifestyles to us and when he does not, we reject him.

The answer is to fast. It is the third great discipline that
Jesus commands us to pursue in our secret places. The
voluntary renunciation of things that are good for the sake
of relationship with God and participation in his kingdom
dream. The only way to stop the consumerist merry-go-
round is to stop.

Fasting is often thought of in relation to food but the
principle is much wider. Sometimes fasting is going without
something – food, TV, books, whatever – in order to make
space to pursue God. Sometimes we fast from those things
that seem to be becoming too important to us. Paul said,
'Everything is permissible for me – but not everything is
beneficial. Everything is permissible for me – but I will not be

mastered by anything' (1 Cor. 6:12). There are some things in our lives that are becoming so important that they have begun to have a detrimental effect on us, and our relationships with God and others. They have begun to master us. It may be food, sex, shopping, designer clothes, worship albums or work! Fasting is the answer because it helps us to reassert control and re-establish our true priorities.

We have been under a stealth attack. Things that we have not seen are destroying our lives with God. We are swimming around in an ever-warmer pan of water not realising that we are dying. We have had a blind spot. We have been blinded by the three great temptations of our age – independence, consumerism and the love of money. Jesus calls us to the better way of the three great disciplines of prayer, giving and fasting.

All of us are responsible for our own secret places. What we fill them with, the values we hold there, the thoughts we indulge there, and the fantasies we play out there. It is there, in the secret place, that the Father looks. He looks not to judge and condemn but to reward and welcome. The rich man had a choice between treasure on earth and relationship with Jesus and participation in his kingdom dream. He went away sad. We also have to choose.

How Then Shall We Live?

Of course, some of us are dissatisfied. We have an ever-increasing sense that things are not right. We are working harder but feeling worse. We have collected all the 'stuff' that should make us happy but feel instead a kind of anxious emptiness. We are aware that the water we are swimming in is getting hotter and we are beginning to feel uncomfortable. We just don't know what to do.

This is where we want a list of do's and don'ts. But there are no rules. There is just relationship. There is no definitive list of what to do; there is just the struggle of working it out with God and others. There is no 'one way' to build a strong relationship with God – no set of rules about what you can buy and what you cannot. There is just a commitment to follow Jesus and work it out with him and his other disciples, as we walk with God.

It starts with the secret place and the decisions that we make there. Will I develop a strong, intimate, personal relationship with God? Will I make time to speak with him, listen to him and worship him? Will I pray, 'Your will be done' and so align my desires to his?

In his power and strength, and only in relationship with him, can we begin to think through giving and fasting.

I am often asked how I decide what to buy. People are generally looking for a set of rules. This car is OK. That one isn't. This much for a coat is godly, that amount is not. I have already said that there are no rules, just an honest seeking of God for wisdom. It is also helpful to talk things through with others. We have been taught that our money is our private affair and no one should tell us what to do. We have seen that our money is intimately tied up with our discipleship and walk with God. We are happy to talk through all kinds of discipleship issues with others, why not our spending, saving and borrowing? This will keep us honest and help us to build a community of people who are seeking to follow God in these areas.

I have three principles in my attempt to follow Christ in these areas:

- Stewardship
- Simplicity
- Ethics

Stewardship

This is the strand of teaching in the Bible that says that my money and wealth does not belong to me but to God. I just look after it for him and his purposes. This means that I must spend it on things that please him. It also means that I must use it wisely. This might mean that buying a better quality product that will last a long time is better than buying a much cheaper product that will need replacing more quickly. It is about being prudent in saving and spending. It is also about spending money on God's priorities.

Jesus presumes that we will be giving. It seems wise that we should be giving to our local church and to support God's work in our communities and across the world. We also need to be generous in our interactions with others. We need to view our wealth – money, car, home, etc. – as resources for God and his purposes rather than primarily as our resource. More radically, we should develop the habit of giving away things that have become too important to us. But we also need to get more creative.

You don't need to have money to give things of great value. One of the more curious commands of the New Testament is in 2 Corinthians 13:12, 'Greet one another with a holy kiss.' The point is not about kissing but about greeting. We are busy people, rushing through our lives, so busy that we don't have time to notice the people around us. Or, rather, we notice the people we think are important. The ones that can help us to get what we want, or who are the people we think are cool and who we want to be friends with. But our days are full of other people. Some of them are so close that to us that familiarity really does breed contempt. For these, we need to re-cultivate the ability to give appreciation. Some of them are marginal to our lives. They sold us a ticket for the train or a coffee from the street stall. Yet all of them are fantastically important to God. All of them are made in his image. All of them are people for whom he has dreams, hopes and plans. And he asks us to greet them, to give them a sense of humanity, appreciation and love, to look them in the eye and acknowledge them. We all crave recognition and appreciation. We all desire to be noticed and not just be marginalised – part of the background mood music. All of us can give that gift to everyone we meet. Greet one another.

What about the gift of hospitality? All of us want to belong, to have a place where we are known and appreciated. We talk about the gift of prophecy or preaching, but I am struck with how Jesus seemed to build his ministry on the basis of giving and receiving hospitality. He invited people into his world when he asked them to follow him. This is the heart of hospitality. It is when we say to someone that they are welcome with us. They are part of our world. They matter. It is an act of giving when we do that to people who can in no way repay us. When we do it for people that we do not want to impress or flatter. It is easy to invite people around with whom we want to be friends – people who are attractive, fun and easy. It is harder to be hospitable to the ones who are more socially awkward or who are new or different. Yet this is giving. It is a realignment of our priorities away from that which is simply comfortable for us to a participation in God's kingdom dream. By practising hospitality we can give others a sense of belonging.

We also give when we make choices about our consumption, not just on the basis of price and quality to us, but on the basis of quality of life and pay to the people who made our goods. That is the practical outworking of this book. We have loved a bargain so much that we have forgotten who is paying the price. We need to start giving fair wages to the people who harvest our food and make our clothes.

So the stewardship principle starts with an acknowledgement that all that I have belongs to God and must be used for him and his purposes. It will mean that I give money and things away. It will mean that I spend and save wisely. It will mean that I spend on the activities that God values.

Simplicity

The second principle is that of simplicity. Most of us in the West have too much stuff. We are on the merry-go-round and need to stop. We have houses packed with things we don't use. We consume endlessly. It costs us a fortune and our extravagant lifestyles are costing the earth. Western lifestyles are using too many natural resources and causing pollution. Climate change will be caused by us, but paid for by the world's poorer communities. When the rivers rise or the floods come in the UK we will have defences, emergency services, compensation and support. When the same happens in Bangladesh people will die. God created the earth and asked us to be stewards of it. Our lifestyles are too expensive for the earth.

They are also too expensive for our walk with God. God designed clothes, houses, food and things to serve us, to bless us and help us as we walk with him. As we have been seeing for many of us the 'stuff' has taken over. We cannot stop purchasing and accumulating. We need to stop and live more simply.

This will enable us to release more money for God's priorities, keep our priorities in the right order, free us from the pursuit of things and relieve the environmental pressures on the world as we consume less of the world's scarce resources and contribute less pollution.

There are many ways in which people put simplicity into practice. An easy one is to go through your home and give away everything you have not used for a year. Another way is to only replace things when they have worn out rather than when a new version in a different colour comes along. Another way is to buy things of high quality that will last rather than contributing to a throwaway culture. Or purchase items from charity and second-hand shops or auctions. This recycles, saves money and allows you to develop unique and individual combinations. It is also worth thinking through how to keep the Sabbath. The Sabbath was a day when ordinary activity stopped and people could focus on their relationships with God and others. In our age of twenty-four hour shopping, we need to fast from consuming by practising Sabbath. It might be that you decide not to shop on one day or find other ways to say 'stop' to the consuming passions.

So, the simplicity principle is an acknowledgement that my life does not consist in food, clothes and 'stuff', but in relationship with God and participation in his dream. It involves fasting as a powerful act of renunciation, when we voluntarily forgo some of the 'stuff' in order to reassert the priority of the kingdom dream. And it is an acknowledgement that we in the West need to live more simply so that others can simply live.

Ethics

This strand of teaching is the focus of this book and is spelt out in detail in other chapters. The ethics principle says that I must be concerned about the people behind the products that I buy. That how they are treated and what they earn has to matter to me. That the way that things are produced, the working practices, environmental practices and social activities of the companies matter to God and he is asking us to put our money where his values are.

These three strands sometimes conflict. The most ethical option is sometimes the most expensive. The stewardship argument means doing one thing, the simplicity argument something else. That is why I describe it as a struggle.

We recently bought a new TV. We could have spent anything from £50 to £5000. What would Jesus have bought? Would he have bought a TV at all? We researched the companies to find out their ethical and environmental pedigree. We thought about how much money we had to spend and how much we felt comfortable before God spending. We researched reliability and longevity. We talked to friends. And then we made our choice. I hope that we chose well. I know that the process of thinking it through, of agonizing over a purchase helped reveal our blind spots and question our culture's values, and caused us to reconsider priorities. It helped us to see.

Section Three

FIVE LIFESTYLE HABITS
TO CHANGE THE
NEIGHBOURHOOD

'Nobody made a greater mistake than he who did nothing
because he could only do a little.'
Edmund Burke

When you hear the word 'powerful', who springs to mind?
Prime Ministers? Presidents? Media Moguls? Have you
ever considered yourself? As consumers, we have more
power than we can ever imagine – the power to spend, the
power to choose, the power to make a noise in the high
street, not just on Downing Street.

In the first section of this book we looked at the issues
and injustices that are facing many millions of our global
neighbours working in the food and fashion industry. We
saw how, for many workers in the garment industry, wages
are too low to live on, eighty-hour work weeks are
common, and their health and safety is being undermined.
We revealed how many workers in the food industry also
work long hours for low pay on which they cannot afford
the basic essentials such as education for their children, or
medicines when they are ill. So what can we do to bring
positive change?

137

So what can we do?

In this section we will have a look at how we can connect our faith in a God who is passionate about justice, with our everyday lifestyle choices. We will explore five areas of lifestyle where we can form habits that will have a transformational impact on our neighbours.

The five habits are:

1. Consuming with conscience:
   Putting your money where your faith is.

2. Campaigning for change:
   Speaking up on the high street, not just Downing Street.

3. Communicating with passion:
   Revolutionary conversations in the everyday.

4. Connecting with the poor:
   Choosing to see.

5. Committing choices to God:
   Intimacy with God that impacts the poor.

Each chapter ends with an action guide, with practical tips on what to do and where to look for further information and resources. A fuller list of contact details and information can be found in the directory at the back of the book.

Sixteen

Lifestyle Habit 1: Consuming with Conscience

'Do not underestimate the power of a vigilant consumer.'
Anita Roddick

Putting Your Money Where Your Faith Is

Choosing Fairtrade and ethical products when we shop, and encouraging others to choose them too, is a simple way to adopt practical compassion for the poor into our lifestyles. Stephen Montgomery, a Fairtrade campaigner when studying at Queen's University, Belfast, says, 'I buy Fairtrade myself because I'm a Christian and I share God's concern for the poor. So if I can use the power that being a Western consumer gives me for God's glory by helping the poor, then why not? Buying Fairtrade is a really simple way of doing it.'

Fairtrade does what it says on the label: it guarantees a better deal to producers in the developing world. It works by ensuring that small-scale producers like Adolfo and Isabel, coffee farmers, are paid a secure, guaranteed price for their crops, so that they have the security of knowing that they can plan for their future.

Fairtrade is making a big impact on people's day to day lives, on their futures and on their families.

Adolfo and Isabel are coffee farmers who are passionate about their children. They want to give them a good education. They also want to preserve their close-knit family life on the coffee farm where each child already has his or her own patch of coffee plants. Adolfo and Isabel are members of Coopeldos, which exports part of its crop to the Fairtrade market. For these sales, the couple gets a price guaranteed to cover the cost of production. However, the rest of their crop gets a much lower price. Coopeldos would like to export more to the Fairtrade market, but despite the massive growth in sales of Fairtrade goods, there's not enough consumer demand yet.

Adolfo says,

> I hope consumers will buy more Fairtrade coffee so we can maintain ourselves like this. If it wasn't for Fairtrade with prices so low at the moment, we would get deeper and deeper into debt. I know other producers who are getting into debt, some have to abandon coffee altogether, and then the father goes and seeks work in the city. When that happens, the family is split up. If the family stays together then it protects the children against problems such as drug addiction.

For more than 5 million people worldwide, like Adolfo and Isabel, Fairtrade means better terms of trade and decent production conditions.[39]

The Fairtrade Foundation, which was established in 1992 as the UK member of the Fairtrade Labelling Organisations International (FLO), works with its partners to maintain these standards by regularly inspecting developing world suppliers, checking contracts and trade terms. Fairtrade is

The FAIRTRADE Mark

different to ethical trading. Ethical trading means companies are involved in a process of trying to ensure that the basic labour rights of the employees of their developing world suppliers are respected.

The FAIRTRADE Mark, which applies to products rather than companies, aims to give disadvantaged small producers more control over their own lives. It addresses the injustice of low prices, by guaranteeing that producers receive fair terms of trade and fair prices, however unfair the conventional market is.

The FAIRTRADE Mark is the only independent consumer label that guarantees international Fairtrade standards have been met. When you see the FAIRTRADE Mark on products, it is a promise that the farmers and workers who produced them are guaranteed fair pay, and that both they, and their environment, are treated with respect. Fairtrade ensures a premium for producers to invest in their business and their communities to provide clean water, healthcare, education and a better environment.

Fairtrade is certainly whipping up a frenzy on the high street. Thirty-nine per cent of the British public is now aware of the FAIRTRADE Mark according to a MORI poll, up from 25 per cent last year. In 2003, consumers bought a staggering 2083 tonnes of Fairtrade coffee from shops and supermarkets. Coffee shops sold 385 tonnes of Fairtrade coffee during the same period – that's almost 70 per cent more than the previous year!

'I hope consumers will buy more Fairtrade coffee so we can maintain ourselves like this.' Adolfo, coffee farmer

Over the past three years consumption of Fairtrade foods in the UK has more than doubled. At the beginning of 2004, shoppers were spending over £2 million per week at the checkout on products with the FAIRTRADE Mark. Fairtrade product retail sales for 2003-4 ran at an incredible £100m a year and sales have grown for 40-50% a year.

The British public now drinks 1.7 million cups of Fairtrade tea, coffee and cocoa each day, and eats 1.5 million Fairtrade bananas a week! Nearly all major supermarkets, and many independent stores, now include Fairtrade in their range.[40]

Small Change For Us – Big Change For The Producers

Harriet Lamb, Director of the Fairtrade Foundation says, 'The rapidly rising sales prove that consumers are ready to put their money where their mouth is, and to play their part in creating a fairer world.'

This consumer action at the check-out is great news for the people behind the products. Bulging Fairtrade shopping baskets really are bringing tangible benefits for the farmers and workers in the developing world. Globally, Fairtrade produce is sourced from 422 producer organizations in forty-nine countries, representing approximately 1 million farmers and workers. As a result, over 5 million poor producers and their families in developing countries are seeing change for the better.[41]

Sivapackiam is one of them. Like Durjimoni and Sujan, Sivapackiam works as a tea picker. She lives on a tea plantation in Sri Lanka, is married with four children and is 38 years old. She has been picking tea on the same estate for twenty-three years. It's a hard life. However, Sivapackiam's working conditions and quality of life have changed for the better because she now supplies tea for the Fairtrade market.

Fairtrade Foundation

M. Sivapackiam, Stockholm Estate, Sri Lanka

All workers on tea estates that supply the Fairtrade market have a workers' organisation to represent their interests. In Sivapackiam's case, she represents her fellow workers on a 'Joint Body' that decides the use of the Fairtrade premium. She is excited about the difference this can make:

> A year ago, we didn't have any electricity in our houses. All the members of the Joint Body got together and discussed how we could pay to install it. Some money came from the Fairtrade premium and we each took out a loan. With electricity, my children can study at night. In the morning, I can iron their clothes and we can use a hotplate for cooking. I am happy that Fairtrade helps me support my family.

Sivapackiam is the women's leader on the Fairtrade registered estate where she works. She is passionate about having a voice to represent herself and the other workers. 'Before, we were very afraid to talk to the manager – especially we women. We'd run into the fields when a manager was coming.' Now she discusses issues such as training of the tea pickers with the management. She believes that workers need the opportunity for self-development and an improved salary: 'I think we are making a difference.'[42]

For the best part of forty years, Concepcion Nunez, a banana grower, has lived in a run down village called Juliana, in the north of the Dominican Republic. All of the houses there were built by the company for the workers on their banana plantation. The company supplied running water, a school bus and other vital amenities to attract a workforce in a remote place with no other infrastructure or local population.

However, when the company left in 1962, they took the roofs of the houses with them, devastating the community

Fairtrade Foundation

Concepcion Nunez, banana grower, Dominican Republic

and leaving them with no income. The original buildings have fallen into disrepair and the village is taking on the look of a ghost town. It is clear why Concepcion wants out.

Concepcion began to grow bananas herself in 1994, but it was extremely difficult to find a market in such a poor, remote area of the country.'No commercial exporter would normally come to Juliana,'she explains.'Whatever I earned, I still had debts by the end of every month.'

Since 2000, Concepcion has been selling her bananas to the UK Fairtrade market.'Five respected farmers from our community were organising a group. I joined because I trusted them.'The increase in income allows Concepcion to make savings every month, and the social premiums ensured by Fairtrade have given the community a canteen, a baseball pitch, new housing, and improved water and sanitation facilities. Some other farmers from the community have been able to move out since they started selling their fruit to the Fairtrade market and Concepcion would love to join them. [43]

Pauline Sewa, a cocoa farmer from Ghana, has had a taste of the benefits of Fairtrade too:

> Since my husband died I have had many worries. I have struggled to feed my children, pay for their school. I had no money. Fairtrade and being a member of Kuapa Kokoo co-operative means I have money. It means I can send my children to school, buy new clothes for them and buy a sewing machine to try to make extra income.[44]

There are now over 300 Fairtrade products available from over 150 companies, with shoppers able for the first time to enjoy pineapples, mangoes, and a wide range of confectionery including Fairtrade chocolate cake and cookies.[45] Fairtrade products include many different foods such as cocoa, chocolate, coffee, tea, sugar, bananas, orange and tropical juice, grapes and honey, apples, pears, plums, satsumas, clementines and lemons.

Fairtrade now accounts for nearly 18 per cent of the UK roast and ground coffee market, and Cafédirect is now the UK's sixth largest coffee brand.[46] The Co-op supermarket is really leading the way for Fairtrade. It has not only switched all of its own label chocolate bars to Fairtrade, which has doubled the sales of Fairtrade chocolate, but it also switched all of its own brand coffee to Fairtrade.

Being a consumer with a conscience is not just about what you fill your shopping trolley with to take home. With nearly one in five hot drinks consumed outside the home it is important to think Fairtrade when you are out and about as well. Following Costa coffee's lead in offering their customers a choice of Fairtrade tea and coffee, Starbucks also launched a regular promotion of Fairtrade filter coffee, while Pret-A-Manger switched all their filter coffee to Fairtrade. Many government offices and local parliaments have also switched to Fairtrade.

Don't shop quietly.

> On my recent trip to Africa, I spoke of the need to build a new partnership between developing countries and the developed world. Fairtrade provides an inspiring example of such a partnership. On my visit, I had the privilege of visiting cocoa farmers in Ghana and saw for myself how Fairtrade in cocoa is increasing incomes and empowering local producers operating in global markets.
>
> *Prime Minister, Tony Blair, on his visit to Kuapa Kokoo Union, Ghana, March 2002* [47]

See the directory at the back for a list of Fairtrade products available.

Clothes Shopping for the World

Just like the food industry, the garment industry is big business. In 2002 shoppers in the UK spent over £33 billion on clothes, with a staggering 40 per cent of that total finding itself split between the top four retailers. No wonder over 18,000 glasses of champagne were drunk at London Fashion Week 2003.[48] Anita Roddick, founder of the Body Shop said, 'if trade undermines life, narrows it or impoverishes it, then it can destroy the world. If it enhances life, then it can change the world.' The good news is that there are 'ethical trade' and Fairtrade organisations at work in the UK, trying to make trade work better for the poor, so that the workers can have cause to join in the celebrations.

'Ethical trade' means different things to different people. Some refer to 'ethical trade' as an umbrella term for all types of business practices that promote more socially and/or environmentally responsible trade. Others, such as the Ethical Trading Initiative, use the term in a much narrower sense, referring specifically to a company assuming responsibility for the labour and human rights practices within its supply chain. Ethical trade works within conventional international trade. It tries to ensure that decent minimum labour standards are met in the production of the whole range of a company's products. It is about ensuring workers' rights are upheld throughout the supply chain, by working towards the ending of child labour, forced labour and sweatshops, and looking at health and safety, labour conditions, and labour rights.

Ethical trade calls on high street stores to take responsibility for the people behind the products. It requires them to take steps to commit to ensuring that the people who make the clothes they sell work in safe and healthy conditions, are paid a wage they can live on and have the right to form or join unions so that they can take their own steps to improve their situation. It calls on companies to agree to have codes of conduct. These are rules, which companies have decided they and their suppliers will comply with. To really work, these codes of conduct need to include important labour standards such as the right to form a trade union and the right for workers to get together to negotiate for better pay and conditions. They also need to be checked by people who do not work for the company to make sure that the workers are being treated well.

Ethical Trading Initiative

Some high street retailers are taking steps to ensure that profits are not being put before people. The UK has 30,000 independent garment companies that have less than five stores each, but the top four control over 40 per cent of the UK clothes market. The good news is that out of the top four two have joined the Ethical Trading Initiative (ETI) – Marks and Spencer, and Next. One of the major stores from the third, Mothercare, which is owned by the Storehouse group, has also joined, as well as New Look, Monsoon and thirty other companies. Companies that have joined the ETI are committed to taking positive steps to improve worker's labour standards.

However, the Arcadia group (which has almost 2000 outlets throughout the country and eight brands including Dorothy Perkins, Top Shop/Man, Burton Menswear, Evans, Wallis, Miss Selfridge and Outfit among others), as well as River Island and Oasis are amongst the major high street companies who have not yet joined.

The ETI was set up in the UK by companies, voluntary agencies and trade unions to help businesses work together to take steps to make wages, working conditions and general standards better for workers. It is funded by these members and also receives grants from the UK Government Department for International Development. The members of the ETI want to ensure that the working conditions of employees in companies that supply goods to consumers in the UK meet or exceed international standards.

The ETI has one of the best codes of conduct, which companies can use as their own code. It is one of the best as it includes all of the most important International Labour Organisation standards. Companies that join the ETI commit to taking steps to improving conditions for their workers by adopting the standards that are contained in the ETI Base Code. If this code was adopted and implemented by all high street clothes stores, it could have a positive impact on the working conditions and quality of life for garment industry workers. Here's what the code really would mean for the people behind the products.

Working conditions are safe and hygienic
This means that, amongst other things, steps should be taken to prevent accidents and injuries in the workplace. Workers should have regular health and safety training, and access to clean toilets. Workers' accommodation should be clean and safe.

Child labour shall not be used
This means that no children (anyone under the age of fifteen qualifies as a child unless the local law in the country says a higher or lower age for work or schooling) should be recruited. If children are found to be working in the company, a programme should be set up to enable that child to attend quality education until they are no longer a child. Child labour means work that is done by children younger than the age above, which is likely to be dangerous or to interfere with the child's education.

Working hours are not excessive
Employees should not work excessive hours – usually more than forty-eight hours a week on a regular basis – and should have one day off for every seven days worked. No one should be forced to do overtime or expected to do it on a regular basis, but if they choose to do it they should not

have to do more than twelve hours per week and they should be paid well for it.

No discrimination
Discrimination means being treated differently to others because of factors like race, religion, age, disability, gender, marital status, being a member of a trade union, or your political beliefs. When workers are chosen for recruitment, training or promotion everyone should be treated equally.

Regular employment is provided
This means that there should be legal contracts written up when any work is to be carried out. This is so that people cannot be insecure in their work, not knowing how long they can expect to work for and under what agreement.

No harsh or inhumane treatment is allowed
This means that workers should not be abused verbally, physically or sexually – or intimidated or threatened in any other way.

Living wages are paid
A living wage is a wage that should be enough to meet workers' basic needs such as food, healthcare, education and accommodation. Often a living wage is higher than a country's minimum wage.

Employment is freely chosen
This means that there should be no forced or involuntary prison labour. Workers should be free to leave their employer after a period of notice.

Freedom of association and the right to collective bargaining
Workers should be able to join or form trade unions of their own choosing and to bargain for better wages and working

conditions. Workers' union reps should not be treated badly in the workplace and should be free to carry out whatever duties they have.

Ethical Trade – what does it require of us?

Ethical trade requires you and I to not shop quietly. Clothes retailers listen when we shoppers, their money-spinners, have something to say. When we show concern that most of the money we spend ends up in the hands of companies selling clothes, and not the hands of those who make them, shops listen. One way to find out whether high street clothes stores are taking responsibility for the treatment of their workers is to check if they:

- Have a code of conduct that includes the International Labour standards. (You can check out company websites to see if they do.)
- Allow outside agencies to check if they are putting their code into practice, to assess whether they are really benefiting workers.
- Have joined the Ethical Trading Initiative. (To see which companies have joined check out www.ethicaltrade.org and see the chapters on campaigning and communicating for ideas on how to take action on the high street.)

While we shop, we should congratulate the companies who have joined the Ethical Trading Initiative. It's important, however, to make them aware that customers want to see evidence of how they put their promises into practice, to bring real change for the workers at the other end of the supply chain. It's important for them to be aware that customers really do care about the people who make their clothes and want to see evidence of increased ethical business practice. They also need to know that shoppers are prepared to put their own money where their mouth is and pay more for products to ensure the rights of workers.

What about boycotting?

Boycotting is not usually the answer unless it is one that the workers are requesting themselves.

A boycott could actually be damaging to the livelihood of workers. The reason for this is that if we in the UK stop shopping in a certain store, the lower demand for clothes items may cause factories to close, thereby forcing workers out of jobs. Any job is better than no job for these people, who, without the low income their job provides, would be placed in a more desperate position of poverty. It is much more effective to decide to not shop quietly and to ask questions when you shop, to keep up the pressure on companies to make changes to benefit the poor.

The more customers talk about the issues, the more companies will have to listen. However, if workers decide themselves that they need to have their voices heard and organise a boycott, then they can be effective. Consumers can show their support for workers by writing letters to managers and letting them see that they need to take the issue seriously.

While carrying on your 'don't shop quietly' campaign, you should also support fair trade shops and online outlets so that they can grow and continue to support trading projects to reduce poverty. Both courses of action are essential to bring change. There are many companies who are working hard to put people before profits in the clothes, food and general market.

People Tree

People Tree is a pioneering fair trade and ecology fashion company founded by Safia Minney, a British fair trade and environmental activist. It works with seventy fair trade groups in twenty countries, and has a fair trade policy of paying producers a fair price, in advance when needed, and ordering regularly. The company sells clothing, fashion accessories and a wide range of products via mail order and through fair trade shops throughout the UK.

Safia says,

> I set up a fair trade fashion company because I wanted to wear clothes that were free of exploitation and not toxic, that looked great. I was hoping to achieve a way of reaching the marginalized poor in villages in rural areas in developing countries, and empowering and promoting job opportunities and reviving community initiatives. People say that fair trade is about empowering the producer, but I think it's about empowering the consumer as well, with enough information to use their shopping to change the world … It's a relatively small change for us to buy something through fair trade, but makes a big difference to producers in the developing world.

> The big difference between how fair trade fashion works and how high street clothes stores operate is that fair trade fashion starts with the traditional skills and natural materials of a particular community and region, rather than just looking for where the biggest profits can be made with the least hassle.

> Fair trade fashion is becoming more and more popular because not only are people understanding the problems facing the often very bad working conditions of garment factory workers, and wanting to be sure that the clothes

they buy really support the producer with fair wages, safe working conditions and respect, but also because fair trade fashion now looks really stylish.

Wayne Hemingway, designer and fan of People Tree, puts it this way: 'This is the kind of fashion we need: People Tree designs cool stuff from traditional skills and materials, and does a great job of putting money back where it needs to be.'

Sharpa has been working as a weaver at Swallows Project in Northern Bangladesh for fifteen years. In addition to receiving a fair wage, her sons were able to study at the Swallows school free of charge, which was really important as her husband had died and she was left with the choice of begging or trying to find a job. 'Swallows also gave me interest-free loans and health insurance and yearly bonuses that helped keep me running my home and educate my two boys.' Today there are eighty women producers who work at Swallows, and profits from fair trade cover 50 per cent of the running costs for a school for 300 poor children for the surrounding villages. People Tree is the main supporter of the project. [49]

Safia explains how fair trade is different to the ethical trade that the ETI is working to promote:

The bare minimum for the high street is for manufacturers and retailers to implement properly the Ethical Trading Initiative. Fair trade is different to ethical trade in that it is an alternative approach to conventional international trade. It is a partnership between producers and traders, which aims at sustainable development for excluded and disadvantaged producers in developing countries. Fair trade seeks to alleviate poverty by changing the unfair structures of world trade to help create a fairer society.

People before profits

Tearcraft, the trading arm of Tearfund, provides jobs, fair wages and a new sense of dignity for craft workers in the developing world so that they can help themselves out of poverty. In return the partners emphasize the biblical principles of love, justice and accountability, give priority to the most needy in society, train their group members and are aware of how their work impacts the environment. Tearcraft has brought help and hope to many people living in poverty around the world; people like Kulsum Begum.

The true business figures of Craft Aid therefore lie in the human benefits rather than the financial ones.

Bad working conditions cost Kulsum Begum's daughter her life. Just fifteen years old, she was working on the fifth floor of a garment factory in Bangladesh. On the second floor, someone left an iron switched on and a fire started. Soon the whole factory was ablaze. There might have been some chance of escape, but the caretaker, going to lunch, had locked the doors behind him. Kulsum's daughter was one of those who perished in the flames.

That was five years ago. Two years later, tragedy again struck Kulsum's life, when her husband of twenty-five years died suddenly of a heart attack. He had worked as a caretaker on a building site. While he was alive, their joint income had just been enough to live on. But life does no favours to a fifty year old widow in Bangladesh. 'When I lost my husband,' recalls Kulsum, 'I was working in a factory, but what I earned wasn't enough to survive on. I suffered a lot.'

Kulsum only turned the corner when she got work with Heed, a Fairtrade supplier to Tearcraft: 'I work in a candle workshop in Mirpur which supplies Heed Handicrafts. My job is to pour molten wax into terracotta candleholders, to make candles. I get paid more here than I used to get in the factory.'

Kulsum still has three children at home, but now she is better able to manage. 'With what I earn here, and the money one of my daughters earns, we can support the family. I hope people will buy these things, because the work we do helps to keep my family fed.'[50]

Making clothes with a difference – Craft Aid

Craft Aid is a Fairtrade Tearcraft partner in Mauritius, making furniture, textiles and handicrafts. It aims to provide paid employment to as many disabled people as possible, offering a living wage and a safe and healthy working environment.

The true business figures of Craft Aid therefore lie in the human benefits rather than the financial ones.

Gabriel Kamudu is Craft Aid's Managing Director. He is a Christian who cares passionately about empowering the poor to help themselves out of poverty. The disabled community in Mauritius often struggles to find employment. Gabriel felt called by God to do something to help meet their needs. He says, 'our production activities are carefully chosen so as to be in line with the ability of the disabled person to fit the work. The true business figures of Craft Aid therefore lie in the human benefits rather than the financial ones.'

Naidu and Arvind, two of Craft Aid's employees, helped to produce a range of Fairtrade and organic T-shirts for Tearfund. They are excited about the difference that Craft Aid's fair trade way of working has made to their lives.

My name is Naidu Koomaladevi. I am seventeen years old and I have been dumb and deaf since my birth. I am working in Craft Aid's textile department. When I was sixteen, I started looking for a job, but as I am dumb and deaf it was difficult to get one. I wanted to be independent and stand on my own. I joined Craft Aid in 2002. I feel my personality has changed. I am someone responsible and I am independent. I am happy that I have many friends at Craft Aid.

My name is Arvind Motur. I am thirty-nine years old and mentally disabled. I joined Craft Aid in 1989. I work in the Textile department. Since I have joined I feel that I am developing day by day. I am more respected in society and can approach people much easier than before. I like my job a lot. I am very comfortable at Craft Aid.

Trade that puts people before profits could lift millions of people like Naidu and Arvind out of poverty. It could help to release the chains and break the yoke of many workers around the world, enabling them to fulfil their God given potential.

For a list of ethical companies see the practical action guide below and the list of contact addresses in the Directory.

Action Guide

☑ *Buy Fairtrade products*

Look for the FAIRTRADE Mark if you want to be sure the producers get a fair deal.

FAIRTRADE Mark

It's not just tea and coffee – Fairtrade products come in all shapes and sizes. Look out for Fairtrade products and others that bear the FAIRTRADE Mark on sale at major supermarkets, Oxfam shops, Costa Coffee and by mail order or online shopping from Traidcraft and Equal Exchange. See the directory for a full list of stockists and retail products with the FAIRTRADE Mark.

Fairtrade products are also offered by more than thirty catering suppliers nationwide. For more information visit www.fairtrade.org.uk/suppliers_caterers.htm

☑ *Get informed about companies in the food and fashion industry*

Company websites – most companies have their own websites. These will have information about their ethical policies, or codes of conduct if they have them, so you can see for yourself what the companies value.

Magazines – a growing number of magazines contain updates on alternative Fairtrade and ethical companies, events, campaigns and new products as they are released.

Ethical Consumer gives information on high street company policies and practices, and gives a 'Best buys' ethical rating to well known brands. It also includes news of the latest ethical products.

New Consumer has ethical product updates and reviews, stories about ethical companies, fashion and those who benefit.

Fairtrade Foundation publication, *Fair Comment*, gives updates on Fairtrade products, campaigns, events and news.

The Good Shopping Guide is a leading ethical reference guide listing the ethical level of the companies behind hundreds of everyday consumer brands. It informs you of the simple facts about each company and provides some overall recommendations to help you channel your spending power.

Behind the Label is a US multimedia news magazine and on-line community covering the stories and people of the global clothing industry. It produces resources and a campaign newsletter.

✔ *Look for International standards when shopping*

Look out for these when shopping:

RUGMARK is a global non-profit organisation working to end child labour and offer educational opportunities for children in India, Nepal and Pakistan. The RUGMARK™ label is your best assurance that no illegal child labour was employed in the manufacture of a carpet or rug.

The Good Shopping Guide Logo is a badge of authority that says a brand scored well in the ethicality test which scores their practices in the area of human rights, animal welfare and care of the environment. The logo is already being used as an independent mark of endorsement by several leading brands.

✔ *Buy ethical and Fairtrade clothes*

Don't Shop Quietly. It is crucial that consumers with a conscience keep speaking up for workers as they shop in their local high street clothes stores, while, at the same time supporting fair trade and ethical clothes outlets.

Congratulate shops that have joined the Ethical Trading Initiative over the counter, or in writing, but ask them what they are doing to put their policies into practice. Some of the major high street stores such as Next, Monsoon, Mothercare, New Look, Marks and Spencer, and thirty others have already joined. Check out www.ethicaltrade.org to see who else is in.

Support ethical companies. There are many cool companies who are working to put people before profits, and they need people like you and I to keep buying their clothes so that their excellent work can continue to grow and make an impact. Find out who they are and what they sell by looking at the directory at the back of this book.

Wear your ethics on your sleeve. Wearing funky fair trade clothes opens up opportunities to tell people where you got them and who benefits.

Spread the word. Buy ethical clothes for others, to raise awareness of what is available and who benefits. Why not try it this Christmas, or for the next birthday present?

Subscribe to ethical and fair trade catalogues. There is a growing number of fantastic catalogues, with a wide range of clothes and goods to choose from.

Where to find ethical clothing:

ON THE HIGH STREET

GO Vicinity/ROAD ranges are stocked in a variety of funky clothes stores. All the garments they produce have a 'conscience swing tag' stating that everyone involved in the garment has been paid a decent living wage. The company produces ROAD and GO Vicinity ranges for men and women and has recently introduced a range for young people, Phat Rhythms.

The British Association of Fair Trade Shops (BAFTS) is a network of independent fair trade shops or World shops across the UK. There are over 50 shops to choose from across the UK. Not all of them will sell clothing but have a look in the directory at the back of this book to find which one is closest to you. If you can't find one, check out their website on www.bafts.co.uk where you can shop online or via mail order and catalogues.

The Cred Foundation sells fair trade jewellery. They have a Chichester store and stockists all over the country. Cred are also involved with small community based income generating projects, bringing you a diverse range of goods ranging from Tanzanian batiks hand made by artist co-operatives in Arusha to Ethiopian organic cotton dressing gowns designed by Katharine Hamnett. www.cred.tv

ONLINE ETHICAL STORES

A growing number of ethical outlets are available online. The best place to start is with the one stop shop websites, which link many ethical suppliers together.

Ethical Junction. This site contains a vast array of ethical suppliers and retailers in a virtual ethical shopping centre. www.ethical-junction.com

Getethical.com. Red Pepper and the Big Issue have formed getethical.com. This is a website for buying ethical and green products. Fifty-three per cent of proceeds from the site go to Red Pepper and the Big Issue Foundation, 5 per cent to NGOs and campaign groups, and 10 per cent towards a micro credit scheme set up for the socially disadvantaged.

Fairtradeonline Oxfam and Traidcraft have set up a partnership called Fairtradeonline, which offers a wide range of ethical options including clothes and accessories. www.fairtradeonline.com

Ethical Threads. Their goal is to raise awareness in the merchandising market so that major global artists will find it hard to sell merchandise not verified as ethically clean. Ethical Threads claim that T-shirts bought from suppliers for around 69p are sold to bands at around £17 – making it clear who benefits. Ethical Threads has secured a deal to supply merchandise for Glastonbury. It wants to encourage the government to source workwear for health and emergency services from ethically verified companies. www.ethicalthreads.co.uk

Epona Sportswear. This is the place to look for cool, casual and sports wear. All of their clothing is fair trade and organic, and the company are committed to fairer trade, decent conditions and pay for workers, and respect for the environment.

www.eponasport.com

See the directory for a fuller list of individual ethical and fair trade clothing stockists and companies.

Seventeen

Lifestyle Habit 2: Campaigning for Change

'Speak up for those who cannot speak for themselves, for
the rights of all who are destitute. Speak up and judge
fairly; defend the rights of the poor and needy.'
Proverbs 31:8–9

Speaking up on the High Street, Not Just on Downing Street

Imagine there is a tap filling a bucket of water in front of
you. Your task is to stop the bucket overflowing, and you
have a teaspoon in your hand. What do you do?

Ronald J. Sider describes this test in his book, *Rich
Christians in an Age of Hunger.*[51] An Indian mental
institution used it to establish whether patients were well
enough to go home. If they frantically scooped at the water
with the teaspoon, then further treatment was required. If
they turned off the tap, they could go home.

In the same way, campaigning on behalf of the poor
requires us to tackle the causes of poverty so we can stem
the flow of injustice to the poor. Unless the root causes of
poverty are tackled head-on, efforts to alleviate the effects

are like shovelling water with a teaspoon. Behind every worker's family there are structural injustices, such as legal systems and economic policies that can trap them in an unending cycle of poverty.

Isaiah describes the 'chains of injustice' and the 'cords of the yoke' that bind people to a life of poverty. He also describes compassion and practical help for the poor as the true worship God requires: [52]

> Is not this the kind of fasting I have chosen: to loose the chains of injustice and untie the cords of the yoke, to set the oppressed free and break every yoke? Is it not to share your food with the hungry and to provide the poor wanderer with shelter – when you see the naked, to clothe them, and not to turn away from your own flesh and blood? (Is. 58: 6–8)

Isn't it ironic that we are called to feed the hungry and clothe the naked and yet, today it is the poor who are feeding and clothing us?

Just as Jesus himself stood up for the poor, the marginalised and mistreated, we are called to stand in the gap for those who are suffering: 'I looked for a man among them who would build up the wall and stand before me in the gap on behalf of the land so that I would not have to destroy it, but I found none' (Ezek. 20).

We need to get to the root of the problem for workers in the food and garment industries, so that history doesn't repeat itself for a new generation of Shimas, Rokyes and Sujans.

Campaigning is the process of mobilising people to join their voices together to take action to challenge the powerful to make decisions to help benefit the powerless. It is about tackling the causes of injustice by challenging those structures, policies and practices which serve to keep the poor in poverty. Campaigning can involve anything from writing letters to politicians, signing petitions, lobbying, marches and boycotts, to demonstrations, prayer vigils, publicity stunts and media work. It is directed against a target to achieve a specific result. The purpose of our speaking out against injustice as Christians is to loosen the chains of injustice and bring freedom from oppression for the poor.

In the light of Romans 13, which says that we should submit to governments rather then challenge them, some people don't think that Christians should be getting into political campaigns. However, it is really important to remember that Paul's teaching here depends on those in power responding to God's commands themselves, rewarding good and punishing evil according to his holy standards. But what if those in authority are not governing according to God's laws?

If a government abuses its power and role as a servant of God, Christians have a duty to hold those in power to account for their actions, and to try and encourage them to change their policies and practices to make them more in line with God's ways. There will be many situations when it will be more in line with biblical teaching to challenge those authorities on behalf of those who are suffering than to keep quiet. Moses, Nehemiah and Esther were all used by God to challenge the authorities of the day.

Campaigning is not always confrontational however. MPs, authorities and governments are often aware of problems and can even welcome suggestions to change them. Stephen Timms, a Christian MP, says, 'So much of what the Bible says touches directly on political questions. It's quite hard to look at the Bible seriously and then look at what's happening around us and not want to take an interest in politics at some level or other.'

Looking After Number One

Speaking up on behalf of the poor is fundamental if we are going to obey the 'royal law', which is how James describes God's call to us to love our neighbour as we love ourselves. Why? Well, let's ask the question: how do we love ourselves?

We love ourselves in a million different ways each day. I want to highlight just two of them. First, we love ourselves by making sure our basic needs are met. For example, when we feel hungry, how do we respond? Do we ignore the feeling and hope it will go away? Do we convince ourselves that we don't need to do anything about it – someone else will sort it out? Not a chance. We take action.

Just how hungry do we have to feel before we do something about it? Five minutes? One hour? An afternoon? A day? Not likely. If you are anything like me you will do something about your hunger as soon as you feel a slight nudge of it, because we love ourselves enough to respond to our needs as soon as we are aware of them. We love ourselves enough to be extravagant with the amount of time, money and energy we expend on ourselves. We love ourselves as a matter of instinct.

Secondly, we love ourselves by ensuring that we are treated the way we deserve to be treated – fairly. So, we will speak up for ourselves when things happen in our day that make us feel we have been treated unfairly. Maybe it's a little thing like we are overcharged for lunch at the sandwich shop. Or someone jumps the queue in front of us at the post office. Maybe it's a big thing. Our bank statement is wrong and the bank has charged us massive interest for a loan we have not taken out – how do we respond?

If you are like me, you would tell someone about it immediately. You wouldn't hesitate to speak up about it, to try to rectify the situation. You wouldn't think twice about letting the people who have treated you unfairly know that you are not happy, and that what they have done is not acceptable.

Why will we instantly go to speak to the shop manager if we have been overcharged for a pair of new jeans, but won't think of speaking up about the unjustly low wages that the person who made the jeans got paid?

If we can relate to this discrepancy between how we respond to being treated unfairly ourselves and how we respond when it happens to others – we may need to face the fact that we do not love our neighbour as we love ourselves.

When it comes to being treated unfairly, we don't have to be reminded to do something about it. We don't have to be emotionally blackmailed to take action. We speak up for ourselves without thinking. We do it without hesitation. We do it over and over again throughout every day of every week without ever getting 'compassion fatigue' for ourselves. It is a natural instinct.

We never get compassion fatigue for ourselves.

Imagine what would happen if we really loved our neighbour in this instinctive way? I believe it would change the world. You may not be aware of it, but you are a person of incredible power and influence. You simply have to choose to use it.

Global Influence: Our Dial-up Connection

How are we influential and powerful people?

First, despite its small size, Britain remains a very important player on the world stage with great potential to influence the policy and practices of other nations. In 2005, the UK Government holds the presidency of the European Union and is hosting the G8 Summit. Britain enjoys a potentially significant level of influence over other world leaders and governments.

Secondly, this incredibly influential Government, grants us, the electorate, who give them their power to govern, the freedom of speech and association. So we can speak out against injustice. We have the

We're called to feed the hungry and clothe the naked. Today it's the poor who are feeding and clothing us.

permission and power to choose to stand up for causes we believe in, and petition our Government for change.

If we want to see our MP urgently, we have the democratic right to walk straight into the Houses of Parliament through St Stephen's entrance, at any time when Parliament is sitting, fill in a green card in the central lobby and ask to see them. This green card will be passed to the MP if they can be found and, if they have time, they will come to see us.

This is so far removed from the situation facing many people in the developing world.

For workers in the garment and food industries, their access to powerful people is often restricted. Their struggles cannot be relayed instantly to others, to evoke support or solidarity. The issues they face cannot always be communicated to people in a position to do something about their problem. This is because, as we have seen, many workers face sacking or punishment if they try to speak out to those in power in order to bring change for the better.

Augustine once wrote, 'Hope has two beautiful daughters. Their names are anger and courage; anger at the way things are, and courage to see that they do not remain the way they are.' Our love for our neighbours should generate a sense of unease with the ways things are currently working for them. Unease generated by love, not bitterness. It was this that propelled Christians in the past to take action to tackle injustice. In *The Truth About Westminster*, Patrick Dixon writes,

> In the 19th century – Christians saw slavery abolished, the hours and conditions of work for women and children transformed, employment exchanges introduced, orphanages and leper colonies set up, built and staffed. We can and must do it again! [53]

Campaigning Works

The Jubilee 2000 campaign for the cancellation of unpayable international debt showed how a real difference can be made when Christians bring their voices and their energy and passion together and make some noise about injustice – real people will benefit! Chancellor Gordon Brown said, 'The Jubilee 2000 coalition achieved more standing together for the needs of the poor in one short year than all the isolated acts of individual governments could have achieved in a hundred years.'

When it comes to campaigning for workers in the garment industry, significant progress has been made which shows that consumer pressure really does make a difference. Ten years ago most of the major clothing companies did not have a code of conduct, or ethical policy, and did not talk about ethical issues in their communication with the public. However, since the launch of the European wide Clean

Clothes campaign, a European and international network of organisations of which Labour Behind the Label (LBL) is the UK wing, things have started to change.

Consumer pressure and campaigning has meant that over the past ten years the majority of companies targeted have formulated fairly comprehensive codes of conduct or improved the codes they already had, and many more companies now explicitly recognise the right to join or form a trade union in their code of conduct. But there is still much room for improvement and other companies need to follow suit. Campaigning and consumer pressure is still needed.

Labour Behind the Label is a network of UK groups campaigning to improve the poor pay, employment rights and working conditions of the international garment industry. It conducts *It's time to make a noise on the High Street, not just on Downing Street.* consumer campaigns to put pressure on companies to take responsibility for working conditions. LBL engages in dialogue with companies who are willing to take steps to improve conditions for their workers.

ETI believes that consumer pressure has led to its corporate membership increasing from twelve companies in 1998, to thirty-five at the end of 2003. A large UK retailer told ETI that if they received ten complaints about a particular issue they would do something about it. An 'over the counter' offensive raising concerns about working conditions could really make a difference.

Campaigning isn't only about challenging others, such as decision makers, to make changes so that poor people are treated fairly – it can, and should, also be about changing ourselves – and making sure our lifestyle choices are benefiting the poor. In light of this, lifestyle campaigns like Tearfund's Lift the Label campaign, have been launched. These not only challenge those in positions of power to change their behaviour, but it challenges Christians as consumers to change their behaviour and choices too. It calls on UK companies to put people before profits by joining the Ethical Trading Initiative, and calls on shoppers to put people before prices.

Hannah Rowland, a Lift the Label campaigner, got active on her local high street: 'I sent over ten Lift the Label postcards to different companies, and got a really long written response from some of the companies which surprised me, and really encouraged me to do it again and keep going! I also asked questions about the companies' ethical policies over the counter in a store when I went shopping. Campaigning doesn't take a lot of effort but it can make a massive impact. God has such a heart for justice – in Isaiah 58 God says if you really want to worship me you must live it out in your lives. All areas of our lifestyle should be an act of worship.'

Stephen Montgomery was on the Student Union Council at Queen's University, Belfast. He put forward a motion for the Union to adopt a policy of guaranteed provision of Fairtrade in its facilities, and of active promotion of these goods to its members. This motion was passed! Vic Simms, the local co-ordinator of student net – Tearfund's student prayer and campaigns network, followed up Stephen's first steps. Vic got the campaign group to collect petition signatures and a staggering 2000 people signed it to ask the university to switch to Fairtrade! Vic says, 'this was more people than voted at the student union elections!! We invited the Vice Chancellor, lecturers and catering managers to a Fairtrade breakfast where we presented a Fairtrade proposal and the petition. The Vice Chancellor is very positive about the prospect.'

Each of you should look not only to your own interests, but also to the interests of others. (*Phil. 2:3*)

Speaking out for the poor is not an optional extra for us as Christians. It is our response to God's call for us to 'speak up for those who cannot speak for themselves' and 'love our neighbour as ourselves'. If we are to truly show love for our global neighbours facing injustice, poverty and oppression around the world – then we will demonstrate that love and concern by standing up and speaking out.

Action Guide

☑ *Campaign with others – the power of teamwork*

Prayer and Campaigns groups. Campaigning and working against injustice is not easy alone. It's much better to get together with like-minded people to pray, share ideas and the sense of achievement when you get results! Campaigning must be soaked in prayer if it is ever to make a lasting impact on people's lives. Many organisations and networks have regional groups who meet regularly to pray and campaign. Search the web to find out who does what, where and for whom. The directory at the back will help get you started.

Kate Culver, a member of a Tearfund prayer and campaign group in London called PACT, (Prayer and Action Changes Things) said,

> Before PACT I was always someone who thought about writing letters for campaigns, etc, even planned what I'd write in my head, but never actually put pen to paper and paper to postbox. However, at PACT we looked into a topic together, decided that we should write to the government, and then each wrote a letter there and then together. When I got home from the group I was on a roll and so looked up my MP and then wrote a letter to him as well and sent them both off in the post the next day. When I actually received the responses it was great and filled me with enthusiasm for the next time!

☑ *Campaign on the high street – the power of the consumer*

Clothes stores

Customer Comment Cards. Fill in customer comment cards wherever they are available. Write the following questions on them and hand in to the manager asking him to pass it on to the company CEO. Explain that you would like a written response.

- Where are your products made?
- What steps are you taking to ensure that people making your products work in safe and healthy conditions and are paid a wage they can live on?
- Is your company a member of the Ethical Trading Initiative?

Customer comment cards are like a 'here's one I prepared earlier' campaign resource for customers with conscience. The shops have produced them precisely because they want to hear from their shoppers. When these are filled out and handed in, many companies log the number of requests related to a particular issue. If there are enough comments relating to the same subject, then shops will want to respond to keep the customers happy.

Garment industry campaigns. As many clothes stores don't have customer comment cards, Tearfund's Lift the Label campaign can equip you with campaign resources and information so you can campaign on the high street. See www.tearfund.org/liftthelabel

Labour Behind the Label is a network organisation that produces materials and urgent action mailings for consumer campaigns. See the directory for contact details.

Don't Shop Quietly. Get together with a group and organise a 'Don't Shop Quietly' day of prayer and action. Your group could have a creative prayer night to pray for the workers, the retail companies, other consumers. On the 'Don't Shop Quietly' day, blitz the high street and ask the questions listed under the customer comment card section on the previous page, to the store managers. Keep it friendly. Congratulate those shops that have joined the Ethical Trading Initiative, but ask them to tell you what action they have taken as a result of joining. This will show them that it is important for customers that they put their words into action.

Food stores/supermarkets/restaurants/coffee shops

Customer Comment Cards. Always fill in a customer comment card when you visit the shop. If it is a supermarket, ask at the customer services desk for one. Coffee shops and restaurants have them at the counter. If the store doesn't stock any Fairtrade items: Ask why they don't, and tell them about the benefits it would bring to producers and shoppers alike if they did. If they do stock some Fairtrade products, congratulate them. However, always ask them to expand the range to include any items that they are not stocking.

Get to know the manager. Become someone whose name and passion for the poor the staff and managers know. It's so vital that you are communicating in a positive, non-confrontational way so that it is clear that you are motivated by concern for the workers, not by anger towards the business. This positive approach will be much more constructive and conducive to good relationships and dialogues than negative nags. So keep it friendly.

Fairtrade Fortnight. Each year, in the first two weeks of March, the Fairtrade Foundation promotes Fairtrade Fortnight. This is a fantastic time for everyone who cares about the people behind the products to join forces and make the FAIRTRADE Mark famous on the high street and in the media. It's all about telling people what it means and letting them sample the delights of Fairtrade products themselves.

People up and down the country in their school, university, church and workplace organise stalls, events, prayer events, campaigns and publicity stunts, and get national and international tongues wagging about the wonders of Fairtrade. Check out the Fairtrade Foundation website for an action guide for this year's Fairtrade Fortnight plans.

Travel Agents

Even when booking a holiday, you can speak up on behalf of the poor. Tourism has an enormous impact on the lives of people living at the receiving end, whether for good or ill. Use your voice to demonstrate your concern for the poor to the travel industry. Travel agents have great access to and influence with tour operators who provide the holidays.

Over the counter. Ask your travel agent if they have any information on how holidays to poor countries affect the local people. When asking your travel agent, the simplest way to raise a concern is to choose one country or continent and ask, 'Do you have any information on how holidays contribute to local development, particularly in Africa, Latin America or Asia? I'm concerned to know the impact of holidays to these places, especially on the local people and environment.'

Ask if the company has an ethical policy? Does this holiday harm or help the local people and economy?

Most travel agents will not have any information – please ask them to take this issue up with their head office and the tour operators they work with – tell them you will call back in a fortnight for a reply.

Tourism Concern. They campaign for ethical and fairly traded tourism that does not adversely affect the planet or communities. As well as raising awareness through campaigns, it has a list of tour operators who take such issues seriously.

See the directory for a fuller list of contact details and resources.

The bank

Some traditional high street banks, through their commercial trading divisions, could be directly financing the arms trade or investing in companies that damage the environment. That's why it's good to think responsibly about whom to bank with.

The Co-operative Bank was the first high street bank to promote itself as an ethical investor. The Co-op Bank has socially responsible values, and they ensure that their investments support the principles of the Universal Declaration of Human Rights. In line with this, they will not invest in (1) any government or business that fails to uphold basic human rights within its sphere of influence; or (2) any business with links to the State in an oppressive regime where its presence is a continuing cause for concern.

smile is an ethical Internet bank that is part of The Co-operative Bank group. They have a strict ethical policy, which means your money will never be invested in unethical organisations.

Triodos Bank is a social bank lending exclusively to positive social and environmental enterprises in areas like social housing, organic food and farming, as well as Fairtrade.

Triodos Fairtrade Saver Account has been developed by the Fairtrade Foundation, and the account offers savers the chance to support the Foundation and some of the UK's most effective fair trade businesses while enjoying a healthy rate of interest.

Ethical investments. Make a list of the ethical issues that you value. Contact EIRIS –the Ethical Investment Research and Information Service. There are now over fifty ethical funds in the UK to choose from. The Ethical Investments Group offer a list of such funds for you to choose from if you are thinking about investing a lump sum. Transfer current investments into ethical funds. Make the switch so your money makes less damage.

Spread the word. Work to see that your work and church or university become ethical investors – raise the issue at relevant meetings so that change can be made for the better.

✔ Campaign at school, university, church or the workplace

Speak up. Send a letter or campaign card to the catering or shop manager. Ask them to switch to Fairtrade products, or expand the range they offer. Tearfund's Lift the Label campaign equips you with materials to campaign for Fairtrade products to be available in your university, school canteen or shop.

Become a Fairtrade church. Tearfund and the Fairtrade Foundation have produced a poster-style certificate for display in all churches that meet the official Fairtrade accreditation criteria. The criteria are easy to meet. All your church needs to do to become an official Fairtrade church is:

- Use Fairtrade tea and coffee for all meetings for which it has responsibility.
- Move forward on using other Fairtrade products, such as sugar, biscuits and fruit.
- Promote Fairtrade at events during Fairtrade Fortnight – and through other activities.

  Email campaigning@tearfund.org for more details.

✔ *Letter writing – the power of the pen*

'The pen is mightier than the sword.' It's a well-known phrase. But what on earth does it mean? Well, in the campaigning world, it's a well-known fact that a letter can be a powerful weapon. In fact, a personal, handwritten letter is one of the most powerful ways in which to voice concern in Westminster. This is because the first job of any MP is to represent, listen and respond to the people who live in their constituency.

Write to your MP. Unlike other mail, any letters that are sent by constituents will almost certainly be read and have to receive some kind of reply. As every single one of us belongs to a constituency, we each have the right to air our views to our MPs. Not just on local matters, but on wider policy issues too. If you write a letter asking your MP to raise an issue with a Minister, then the MP is duty-bound to do so. The Minister is duty-bound to reply in writing to the MP, who then has to write back to the constituent.

Many MPs still gauge the strength of public opinion on an issue by how many personal letters they receive from their constituents on the subject. MPs have told campaigning groups that for every letter they receive, they consider it to represent the views of at least 100 people who probably didn't get around to expressing their views in writing. A simple, short, polite letter, with a concrete ask of the MP, such as asking a question to a Minister, or signing an Early Day Motion, can be very effective. To find out the name of your MP check out www.locata.co.uk/commons or call: 020 7219 4272. Write to: [Your MP's name], House of Commons, London SW1A 0AA.

Sam Moore, a Tearfund campaigner in Northern Ireland, started a letter writing campaign to members of the Northern Ireland Assembly when he discovered that they did not use fairly traded tea and coffee in Stormont. He drafted a letter and collected hundreds of signatures from members of his Christian Union. Weeks later, he was invited to the Assembly to witness the launch of the new Fairtrade catering policy. Result!

Write to the Prime Minister. All international trade needs to work for the poor, not against them. Ask the government to support the aims of the Trade Justice Movement, which calls on world leaders to rewrite the rules of international trade. See www.tradejusticemovement.org

Write to the CEO of your favourite clothes companies. The customer service department should give you their contact details. Check out www.ethicaltrade.org to see if your favourite company has joined the ETI.

Tell them that you care about the people who make your clothes, and you would like the company to consider joining the Ethical Trading Initiative as a positive first step in the right direction. If they have already joined, thank them for doing so but ask them what practical steps they have taken as a result.

Always write your name and address on the letter and ask for a written response.

If you want some tips on what to include, look out for current letter writing and postcard actions on the issue from Tearfund's Lift the Label campaign www.tearfund.org/liftthelabel

Write to the decision makers in your school, university, church or workplace. Write a personal letter to the catering or shop manager or the head of the institution or business you want to ask to switch to Fairtrade. Tell them the benefits it will bring to workers and producers in the developing world.

✔ *Creative petitions – the power of the people*

Creative petitions, if well planned, designed and delivered, can be a great tool to raise public awareness about an issue. They are accessible to people of all ages. A creative petition can often catch the attention of the public and the media as it can be a fun and interactive way for people to connect with a seemingly dry or complicated issue.

Present it to the press. Accompanying a presentation of a completed petition, with a well-written, concise press release, can help to secure media coverage. This can really help to generate greater interest in and awareness of an issue and others may get involved as a result!

✔ *Media and publicity stunts – the power of the press*

Write a Press Release. One positive Christian item printed in a local newspaper or broadcast on a radio station could reach tens, if not hundreds, or thousands of people. A news release is the means by which the media prefer to receive information. Here are some tips on how to put together a news release:

- Use headed notepaper, but mark it with NEWS RELEASE and also the date of dispatch.
- Type, don't handwrite. Use short sentences and paragraphs. Keep to one side of A4.
- Include the most interesting angle of your event in the first paragraph.

- Make sure you have answered the What? Who? When? Why? How? Where? questions in your opening paragraph.
- Include a direct quote from the organiser/spokesperson for the event.
- Invite reporters and photographers to your activity.
- Make sure a contact person is available both during work and in the evenings.
- Check all facts for accuracy with event organisers before sending to the media!
- Send the news release, by mail, or fax, a good fourteen days before the event.
- Phone a few days after mailing to see if they have received your news release and to gauge their level of interest.

Write a letter to the editor. An effective way to get a campaign into the national media without paying for advertising space is through a letter to the editor. On any given day, it has been estimated that letters from interest groups will make up about a quarter of all letter pages in newspapers. The chances of a letter being published will increase if it responds directly to something that has featured in the newspaper. And also if it is short! It makes sense to try to communicate one point strongly, rather than covering a lot of ground because it is up to the editor to cut the letter however he chooses. Look at the letters pages to see what types of letter the paper seems to prefer to print.

Organise a publicity stunt to raise awareness. Think of an outrageous idea that would get people's attention as they walk by, and will get the local media interested. One keen campaigner in Dublin went to extreme measures and dressed up as a giant Fairtrade tea bag! Find a spot that is prominent and busy – where other people are bound to notice you. Send a press release to the local papers and radio station.

Write an article or feature for the local media or newsletter. Contact the editor of your university or church magazine or newsletter and ask if you can write an article about an issue such as the situation of the people behind the products in the food or fashion industry.

If writing about the food industry: Start with some facts and stats about the food industry, and a personal story to show how Fairtrade affects people's lives. The aims of the article in the case of Fairtrade food should be to raise awareness of:

- The FAIRTRADE Mark.
- The impact of unfair trade on people's lives.
- How Fairtrade benefits the poor.
- What items are available?
- Where you can buy them locally.

If writing about the fashion industry: Start with some facts and stats about the garment industry and a personal story to highlight the issues facing the people behind our products.

The aims of the article in the case of the fashion industry should be to raise awareness of:

- The impact of unethical trading on worker's lives.
- How joining the ETI could benefit workers.
- How to take action.

✔ *Online campaign networks – the power of the PC*

Company websites. Use the company website 'contact us' customer comment email facility to ask the company questions.

Online action – many organisations and networks have websites where you can send an instant email message to a decision maker to campaign about an issue. These are quick and simple to do. Tearfund has a number of online campaigning networks where you can get up to the minute prayer and campaign news and actions.

Tearfund's prayer, campaigns and lifestyle networks for students, young people and youth leaders.

student net:	for students and young adults (18–22)
youth net:	for young people (11–18)
network engage:	for youth leaders

Members receive regular email action updates giving urgent prayer and campaign info and actions on the Lift the Label ethical lifestyle campaign, debt, sustainable living and trade campaigns. Visit www.tearfund.org/youth

Tearfund globalaction. Globalaction highlights key campaigning opportunities through a quarterly publication, with additional email news, updates and emergency action requests.

Visit www.tearfund.org/campaigning/globalaction

Email signature. Why not tag on a brief message about an issue or campaign, with a web address, to your email signature. This way, every time you send a message to someone, they will find out about the campaign, and may explore it for themselves.

☑ *Getting to know your MP – the power of the persistent*

MPs are very well connected people. They can ask questions in Parliament, table bills, and can raise awareness of an issue to other members within their party. On a local level, MPs usually have direct influence on local business people, community leaders or councillors.

Most MPs will have a 'constituency surgery' or advice session once a week or a fortnight, usually on a Saturday. This is a great opportunity for people who live in the area to meet the MP, ask them questions and raise concerns. There are campaigners who are dedicated to using these surgery hours to speak up for poverty and justice issues with their MPs on a regular basis throughout the year.

Why not find out when your MP's surgery hours are, and decide to pop along to chat with them, say twice a year. It's always a good idea to get informed about the issue you want to raise before going, so you can present a good case. Campaigning organisations will give you a clear idea of the issues to raise and the questions to ask.

Why not arrange to meet your MP in the next month? Ask him or her to ask the Government what it is doing to make companies more accountable for the treatment of their workers, and to make international trade rules work for the poor. For more information on how to campaign for fairer international trade rules visit www.tradejusticemovement.org

Panel debate. Why not invite your MP, either on his own, or with a number of supermarket or area shop managers to come to your church, university, school or workplace for a panel question time debate on the issue of workers rights and labour standards across the food and fashion industry?

✔ *Mass actions*

People power can make things happen. When large numbers of people get together to walk, demonstrate, lobby or petition on one day, in one location, it can have a really positive impact.

The Trade Justice Movement is a fast growing group of organisations including aid agencies, environment and human rights campaigns, Fairtrade organisations, and faith and consumer groups.

In 2002, more than 12,000 campaigners put trade justice high on the political agenda when they converged on Westminster for the biggest ever mass lobby of Parliament. More than half the MPs in Parliament – 346 in total – were lobbied by constituents who travelled from all parts of the British Isles. The lobby was a great success. 288 MPs signed an Early Day Motion supporting the trade justice campaign. It prompted the Government into talks with representatives of TJM organisations, with briefings to the Prime Minister, Chancellor of the Exchequer, Secretary of State for Trade and Industry and Secretary of State for International Development.

The movement is supported by more than fifty member organisations that have over 9 million members. Together, it is campaigning for trade justice – not free trade – with the rules weighted to benefit poor people and the environment. It organises mass actions, to get the Government's attention and bring policy change. The goal of the Trade Justice Movement is fundamental change of the unjust rules and institutions governing international trade, so that trade is made to work for all. It also calls on the Government to make laws that stop big business profiting at the expense of people and the environment. To add your voice to current actions and mass campaigns, check out www.tearfund.org/campaigning or the Trade Justice Movement site on www.tradejusticemovement.org

Eighteen

Lifestyle Habit 3:
Communicating with Passion

'The passionate are the only advocates who always persuade. The simplest man with passion will be more persuasive than the most eloquent without.'
Rene Descartes

Revolutionary Conversations

We bumped into the Beckhams in London. It was close to Christmas. It was just outside Harrods. They stepped out of an enormous tinted-windowed car and onto the footpath right in front of us. Within seconds, before you could say Sven Goran Eriksson, they, and therefore we, were completely surrounded by people.

Hovering menacingly like flies round a honey pot, the crowds held their mobile phones aloft, straining to take a picture of the delightful duo. They frantically called friends and families, to chatter passionately about their celebrity spot.

The excitement in the air was infectious. Despite not being a Beckham fan, I am ashamed to confess that I got swept away in the moment and joined the communication carnival. I phoned my niece Hannah and texted some friends to tell them who I was looking into the bouncy blond ponytail of. How sad. How tragic. How telling. Within seconds of the Beckhams being spotted, without a second thought, streams of words and images were instantly relayed to spread the word that they were in town. The news travelled unbelievably fast. With each passing minute, masses of people flocked to the sacred spot to herald the arrival of the pair.

On the same stretch of footpath sat a homeless busker. He was in the crowd's field of vision, yet no one seemed to see him. They were distracted. Their attention was diverted. He might as well have not been there at all. He was, to all intents and purposes, invisible.

It made me think.

What happened on that stretch of footpath is a symptom of the tunnel vision that Western culture is often prone to. In the middle of the 'communications revolution' we enjoy today, it is the poor who remain as unconnected and 'out of area' as ever. There is so much 'stuff' that vies for our attention in the whirlwind of social life, family life, friendships, work, church and relationships, that we are simply not aware of the reality of life for people who fall outside the radar screens of our immediate experience.

Communication in Jesus' day was just a tad less fast paced and sophisticated than it is today. However, despite the context that Jesus was moving in, he managed to usher in his own communications revolution without any help from Microsoft, Orange or any other multinational.

Jesus' conversation was revolutionary. He chose to talk and connect with people who others didn't communicate with – the excluded, the poor, the vulnerable and the sinners. His everyday chats and encounters had a transformational affect on the receivers. His words were counter cultural. They challenged the norms and 'acceptable' practices of the day. They confronted the injustice of those who were seemingly 'respectable' and outwardly 'religious'. His conversations signalled a message of hope to people who had only known despair. His communication transmitted a radical message of good news to those who felt forgotten.

Martin Luther King used the term 'wind changers' to describe people who, by their everyday conversation, challenge the values, priorities and perceptions of the cultural climate around them. People who challenge the direction that others may be moving in, by putting fresh ideas into conversations, and modelling counter cultural behaviour that challenges what is considered to be the norm.

Jesus' conversations were 'wind-changing' in the extreme, challenging people to think in a fresh way about things that they had never questioned before. He redefined greatness to mean service. He talked of being first in terms of being last. His conversation over meal tables, on the street, on the hillsides and in everyday settings challenged people to see things differently, challenged people to think differently, challenged people to live differently.

The New Communications Revolution

We too can become wind-changers. People whose words, actions and everyday choices challenge others to remember the poor. We not only need to draw the attention of the powerful to the problems facing the poor. We must bring the reality of life for the poor into our society's field of vision. We can do this if we understand that campaigning is not just about letter writing and petitions, but it should be a lifestyle habit that becomes a feature of our everyday conversations. Amazing things could happen if we were committed to 'Speak up for those who cannot speak for themselves, for the rights of all who are destitute. Speak up and judge fairly; defend the rights of the poor and needy' (Prov. 31:8–9) in our everyday chats and encounters.

It is about making a conscious choice to speak up for the poor in the everyday moments of our daily lives.

We could be wind changing through our everyday interaction with friends, families, or colleagues at work – opening people's eyes to see the poor in their day, making choices that have a positive impact on the poor to encourage others to do the same.

Your life intersects with a unique set of people. If you were to count the number of people who you come into contact with, even in one week, through email, phone calls, conversations and everyday contact, you may be surprised at just how many it is. You live within unique circles of influence – friendship circles, family, work colleagues, sports club members, home groups, people in your neighbourhood and in your email address book. There are people who only *you* have contact, conversations and relationships with, people who you can help to see how their lifestyle choices could have a positive impact on the poor.

The everyday conversations and encounters we have with the people within our circles of influence, could make a difference to the sense of isolation, which Shima, working in her factory in Bangladesh, feels on a daily basis. The text messages we send every day to friends could also be used to improve conditions for Rokye, as he stitches diamantes onto denim jackets. It's all about how we choose to use the opportunities each day presents us with to speak up on behalf of the poor. It's about choosing to use the communication channels we have at our disposal to tell *their* stories, to reveal *their* reality, to profile *their* problems.

It has been said, 'Small stones make landslides happen.' When one small stone starts to shake free of the rest, starts to move, starts to gather momentum, then others around it will begin to do the same – with astounding results!! The things that we choose to communicate, on an everyday basis, could have a much more far-reaching impact than we think.

The Fairtrade Foundation, for example, have benefited greatly from the power of passionate people who have passed on their passions to others! Sales of Fairtrade food products rocketed over the last few years, not by advertising on TV or expensive billboards – but mainly by word of mouth!! People passionate about Fairtrade really have become 'wind changers'– using their everyday conversations to encourage their friends and families to buy Fairtrade, and it is achieving amazing results! The Fairtrade Foundation say that since the first coffee jar bearing the FAIRTRADE Mark hit the shelves ten years ago, a quiet revolution has taken place. This one product has grown to a range of 300! This 'quiet revolution' has happened because passionate people have refused to stay quiet about the things they care about! Four out of every ten people in the UK are now aware of the FAIRTRADE Mark. Every week more and more people are realising they can make a positive difference to the lives of farmers and workers in the developing world.

A lot has been achieved in the last decade, but this is only just the beginning. Fairtrade foods and ethical goods still only account for a small proportion of our weekly shop. To reach more farmers and workers, there need to be more shoppers. To reach more shoppers, there need to be more 'wind changers' – passionate people with an itch to spread the word. 'Once people start buying Fairtrade goods they get hooked. More shoppers buying Fairtrade goods, means more producers are getting a living wage,' says Joy McKnight, a Tearfund campaigner.

If we want to help others see the people behind our products then we must use the everyday channels of communication that are open to us, to tell *their* stories. To let *their* voices be heard. To let people see *their* faces. To open people's eyes to the reality of life for the people who make our everyday life possible.

Small stones make landslides happen.

Imagine what momentum would gather if we naturally, out of instinct, spoke up for the poor in our everyday chats – bringing their names up in conversation; chatting about Sujan the tea picker, as we're having a cuppa; texting our friends for Sujan and Durjimoni, telling them about Fairtrade Fortnight, and inviting them to an event; lifting the labels on clothes and explaining why, as we shop in the high street; making a conscious choice to speak up for the poor in the everyday moments of our daily lives, over coffee, at the checkout, in the changing rooms. It is about doing what we can to help others realise that the choices they make at this side of the world can have a positive or negative impact on people living on the other side.

Imagine the landslide if speaking out for the poor was as natural, and instinctive, for us, as saying 'that's not fair' when we are mistreated.

Imagine the landslide if we spoke as much about the needs of the poor as we do our own.

Imagine the landslide if we chatted to our friends as much about the poor as we do about ourselves.

Imagine the landslide if we changed the climate of conversation and consuming so that bringing the poor into the equation was second nature.

Small stones maybe. But small stones make landslides happen.

Action Guide

Spread the word...

 *Over coffee*

Have a Fairtrade coffee break. Buy Fairtrade products such as tea, coffee, sugar, chocolate or snack bars for friends or family this week and have a Fairtrade coffee break. Let people see just how great it tastes!

 *At the weekend*

Throw a Fairtrade party. Stock up on Fairtrade goodies. At the start of the night you could give a three minute chat about what Fairtrade is, why it makes a difference and which food products are available. Have a tasting time where you pass around different things. It could be blind tasting where people have to guess, from the taste, which products are Fairtrade and which aren't. Have lots of catalogues, food and goodies arranged in a funky way to sell. Have posters and leaflets that people can pick up, read and take away.

 *At Christmas, birthdays and special occasions*

Your presents could open your friends and families eyes to Fairtrade and ethical shopping – and get them talking. Many organisations listed in the directory have catalogues, and online shops from which you can choose a vast variety of funky ethical gifts, cards and clothes and all sorts of other goodies.

✔ *At your church, university, school or workplace*

Notice boards. Get permission to use a board regularly to tell people about issues, events, actions, campaigns that they can get involved in. Hannah Rowland, Tearfund student net campaigner at University College London says, 'I'm living in halls at UCL, and we put up Fairtrade posters up in the kitchens, and stuck Fairtrade leaflets, and even a tea bag – up on the notice board! People looked at it and really got talking about it! It's so good to be able to do something, because sometimes you don't know where to start – the problems seem so big.'

Just ask for a slot. Ask the leader of your Christian Union cell or church for a short slot in the meeting to tell people about the issues facing people behind the products.

Ask if you can give a five minute presentation during the meeting:

- Give people the low-down on the issues facing food and/or clothing producers.
- Use the producer stories in this book to show how trade
- Tell people which Fairtrade products and ethical clothing is available and where they can get their hands on it.
- Use prayer resources on the issue and get people praying.
- Have resources and information available for people to take away afterwards.

Go the whole hog and have a 'Lift the Label' service. Challenge your church to get active. Ask your minister for a meeting devoted to the issue which could include:

A biblical overview of God's heart for the poor.

A presentation of the issue facing the people behind our products.

Prayer for the issue.

Have a stall at the back of church to display campaign resources and information and hand out free Fairtrade samples of tea and coffee.

Offer to run an awareness-raising event. This could be anything from a Fairtrade tasting session, a panel debate on the issue, a global cafe with a band and Fairtrade stall selling gifts and food, to a Fairtrade fashion show.

Set up a Fairtrade stall in your church, university, school or workplace. Zoe Caals co-ordinated a weekly Fairtrade stall in Warwick Students' Union. 'Response from students has been very positive. It's an excellent opportunity to let other students know how easy it is to take a stand against injustice. It's so easy to be stuck in a bubble and not see how little choices in our lives can affect others. The Union is an ideal venue for this sort of action as you can talk to students directly.'

- Ask permission to set up a table and stand in a prominent position, at a time when it will be busy.
- Choose a place where people normally hang around to chat, relax and have coffee.
- Contact the Fairtrade Foundation and other organisations for information leaflets etc. to hand out.
- Read these leaflets yourself so you can answer questions about Fairtrade and can explain what it means.
- Offer people the chance to taste and buy Fairtrade products.

✔ *Put on a 'Lift the Label' global café music night*

Pick a local café or venue with kitchen facilities where people hang out regularly.

Get together some musicians who can play mellow guitar music or DJ to create a chilled out atmosphere. Theme the room with candles and drapes to make it cosy.

Put posters and leaflets and information on Fairtrade products and ethical trade around the walls and on tables. Serve up Fairtrade drinks and snacks.

Intersperse the night with a brief presentation on the issues facing the people behind our products in the food and clothing industries. Let people know about the impact of unfair trade on people's lives, how Fairtrade and ethical trade make a difference, where and what they can buy, and why as a Christian they should care about the issue. Give them a tangible campaign action.

If you know people who have travelled to countries that have been affected by unfair trade, interview them about their experiences and the issues facing the people there.

Nineteen

Lifestyle Habit 4:
Connecting with the Poor

'We never wanted to be considered detached spectators.'
Martin Luther King

Choosing to See

Our God does not watch us from a distance, or keep us at arm's length. He is a God who connects intimately with humanity. In sending Jesus, he 'became a man and dwelt amongst us' (Jn. 1:14), or, as *The Message* puts it, became 'flesh and blood and moved into the neighbourhood'.

In becoming man, Jesus took time to learn our language and heartbeat. But it was not enough for God to send Jesus to become a man. He sent Jesus to *serve* men, including the very least of them – the ones who even the other humans had chosen to reject. Jesus stayed connected to the poor, the excluded, the marginalised, the vulnerable and the forgotten. He spent time eating with them, talking with them, praying for them, reaching out to them. He turned towards the marginalised woman at the meal table. He reached out to the forgotten blind beggar on the street. He spoke up for the woman caught in adultery. 'The poor heard

199

him gladly' (Mk. 12:36). Jesus spoke the language of the poor, using images and phrases they could relate to and understand.

Jesus' life is to be our model. He lived alongside the poor and shared their meal tables, their stretch of dusty road. He gave his time, his love, his compassion. We are called to do the same.

In Isaiah 58 God calls us to 'spend ourselves on behalf of the hungry'. We are to give and give and give until we can't give any more. He calls us to 'satisfy the needs of the oppressed.' We are to give and give and give until they can't receive any more. This is clearly not a call from a God of the token gesture or of the one-off action or of the prayer hit-and-run.

It is a call from a God who spent his whole life outpouring his love. He calls us to do the same.

In *Money, Sex and Power: The Challenge of the Disciplined Life*, Richard Foster challenges Christians to see that the key to living a lifestyle of Christ-like compassion is to 'Reduce the distance between yourself and the poor.' [54] There is a real danger that we can become so comfortable and sheltered, surrounded by like-minded people, pleasant surroundings, a busy job, and an enjoyable lifestyle that we simply don't see the reality of life for millions of people around the world.

The truth is that, compared to the majority of the world's population, we are extremely rich. We live lives that the majority of the world's population can only dream about. We rarely if ever acknowledge just how 'wealthy' we are in global terms.

If the world were in a community of 100 people it would look like this:

- 6 people would own 59 per cent of the whole community wealth.

- 80 people would live in poverty.
- 14 wouldn't be able to read.
- 33 would die of famine.
- Only 7 would have a higher education.
- Just 8 would own a computer.

If you've never seen a relative die in a war, if you've never been a slave if you've never been tortured, you are better off than 500 million people.

If you keep food in a fridge, your clothes in a wardrobe, if you have a roof over your head, a bed to sleep in, you are richer than 75 per cent of the entire world's population.

If you have a bank account, you are part of the 8 per cent wealthiest people in the world.

If you can read these words, you are more fortunate than 1 billion people, who can't read at all. [55]

Cocoon with a View?

There is a cultural phenomenon around today which is known as 'cocooning'. People today are living such hard working, fast-paced, hectic, stress-filled lives that they crave a 'cocoon' of comfort, into which they can retreat whenever they want.

This 'cocoon', is often people's homes. Many people now have homes which are so equipped with the latest technology that they no longer need to go outside the front door in order to chat to people, shop, or watch films. It can all be done via the Internet or home entertainment systems. Contact with anyone or anything which is outside the comfort zone of the 'cocoon' can be very limited.

People can be 'cocooned' in a comfort bubble. They can live a life of virtual reality – where the issues, problems and reality of life for many people outside that comfort zone, can remain locked out – beyond the frontier of the front door.

You and I may exist in 'cocoons' of a different kind. Maybe we are 'cocooned' in our comfortable lifestyle – full of the familiar, the safe and the secure. Maybe we are comfortable spiritually in the 'cocoon' of our church, our Christian Union or cell, or Christian job. We feel we are busy doing good stuff, and there is no need or time, for that matter, to change that.

The more connected to God's heart we are, the more God will break our hearts for the things that break His.

What is it that you and I are protected from seeing because of the lifestyle 'cocoon' which we may inhabit?

The Cocoon Test

- How connected to the poor are we?
- How many people who live below the poverty line in this country or overseas do we know by name?
- How many have we invited inside our homes in the last year?
- How many have we helped in a practical way in the last month?
- How many have we come into contact with this week?
- How many have we prayed for or with recently?
- How many of their homes have we stepped foot in?

We need to make choices and form lifestyle habits that ensure that we don't become so distanced from the poor that we don't even see, never mind understand, the reality of their lives.

Who are the individuals who God is calling us to have eye contact with?

Who are the groups of people who God wants to place into our field of vision?

Which are the countries that God may want us to see with our own eyes?

What are the challenging books or articles which make us uncomfortable, but which God is challenging us to put into our pile of things to read?

There are very practical steps that we can all take to help us get more in touch with the poor. We can read books about issues of poverty and injustice, and search the Web for up to date information and facts and stats on countries and poverty and justice issues. Many organisations have regular free magazines to which we can subscribe, to help keep us up to date with events and urgent prayer needs for people, places and situations. But there is much more that we can do.

Connect with the Poor on your Doorstep

Spend time and make friends with people from different backgrounds. Go and spend time in an area of your neighbourhood or city, helping out with projects for those living in poverty. If we don't make eye contact, build connections and feel compassion for our next-door neighbours living in poverty in our own street or city, then how much less likely will it be that we will see, connect with, and feel compassion for the people whose lives are beyond our visibility range?

In *Good News to the Poor*, Tim Chester, who worked as Research and Policy Director at Tearfund, states that current social trend figures suggest that within a twenty minute stroll of the average UK city church there is likely to be 10,000 people.[56] Out of that number, it is estimated that on average there will be:

2700 people living in households without a car.

1700 people living in low-income households.

1200 people living alone.

1100 people with some kind of mental disorder.

1500 people who talk to their neighbours less than once a week.

1280 people caring for a sick relative or friend.

18 pregnant teenagers.

150 contemplated or recent abortions.

250 people who are unemployed.

100 bereavements within the last year.

40 homeless people in temporary accommodation.

15 asylum seekers.

It's amazing what you don't see.

We often only see the people who are just like us. We've got to choose to open our eyes to see the reality for those whose lives look different.

Connect with the Poor Overseas

There is no better way to understand the issues facing people in the developing world than to spend some time there yourself. Many different development agencies, charities and churches organise summer, Easter and Christmas teams. You can go for as long or short a time as you want. Teams vary from two weeks to two years – depending on the time you have available. Some people get a taster for life overseas while on a summer team, and later decide to go overseas for a longer period of time.

Tearfund runs a programme called Transform, which sends teams all over the world to work alongside partner organisations, projects and churches doing development work and evangelism in the developing world. Teams can do anything from projects such as digging wells, building schools, to working in projects for disabled children, or using sport to build relationships with children on the street.

God knows every one of the 1,200 billion people who will earn less than 60p today. (ILO)

Abigail Walker spent a month last year in Uganda, as part of a Tearfund Transform team, building a water tank for the community, and working with the children living there. She says,

> The experience opened my eyes to a completely new culture. It shook up what I think of as normality. I now feel I can make a difference with my holiday time. If you want to go deeper with God and be shaken out of your comfort zone, consider doing an international project this summer.

The action guide at the end of the chapter will give you more information and ideas about going overseas.

Ethical holidays

Rather than going on a team with an organisation, you may choose to travel to a developing country on holiday with your friends or family. To ensure that your holiday enables you to connect with the poor communities in the country and learn about what life is really like in that place, it's best to choose to stay away from the tourist resorts and hotels.

This type of holiday is not usually the one that you see in the travel agent window on the high street. The all-inclusive holiday is growing in popularity within developing countries. To the tourist it seems ideal: no hassles with bills when you get there. But their cash is going straight to the large companies who operate the resorts. The tourists rarely get to meet the local people who may be selling food, souvenirs and other goods, and the local people often don't see the benefit of the money which tourism is generating in their country.

Many companies run special ethical holidays. These are designed to help travellers connect with the culture and communities in a country, rather than simply with the tourist trail and hotspots. One British tourist describes her ethical holiday experience:

> We went in a small group on a holiday to the Ecuadorian rainforest. Our party stayed with the Rio Blanco indigenous community, in a tourists' lodge built by the village, and we visited the forest with villagers as guides. On the final evening we had a special get-together with the villagers. It was one of the best parts of the holiday for me. We ate delicious local food and they played music for us. Then they asked us to sing something to them in our own language. We knew our money was important to the community, but that night we became more than paying guests, we shared friendship. [57]

Living with the Poor

Short-term teams can be a fantastic starting point in building connection with the poor into our lifestyle as Christians. Many who go on such teams connect with the people or a particular place to such an extent that they feel called by God to go back for a longer period of time. A growing number of people are choosing to spend a year in a developing country, and not just before or after university. People of all ages, at different stages of life, are feeling God's call to leave their comfort zone for a year or more, and go to connect with a poor community in the developing world to serve, love and bless.

There is no better way to understand the human face of poverty than to go and live and work alongside people there yourself – living the way local people live, eating the food they eat, walking where they walk, spending time and building friendships.

When I boarded a plane to Uganda, fresh out of university, I had no idea what a transforming effect that year would have on me. Living in Nyaruhanga village with my mission partner Kate, opened my eyes, blew my mind, changed my heart and ultimately the course of my life.

Waking up to the sound of a village school cockerel crowing every morning, carrying gerrycans to the stand pipe to collect water, cooking over a charcoal stove, lighting rooms with paraffin lamps and riding in pick-up trucks with chickens clucking around our feet, quickly opened my eyes to the reality of daily life for the people there. I wouldn't have believed the lifestyle of the villagers in Nyaruhanga if I had read it in a book or seen it on a documentary on TV.

When I think of Uganda now, or see it on the map, I no longer see it simply as a place, but as a collection of people with hopes and dreams, people who love life.

For Kate and I, Uganda now has a face. We see Uganda as the faces of our friends. The smiley faces of our student friends – Provia, Kenneth, Joab and Justus. The loving faces of our teacher friends – Robert, Anne, Irene, Benson, Mr Munyangabo and Chance. The cheerful faces of our teenage friends – Peter John, Mbabazi, Hope, Richard, Gafati, and Musupu.

Sharing that year with the villagers of Nyaruhanga opened my eyes in so many life changing ways. It opened my eyes to the human face of poverty. It made me realise that I am part of a global neighbourhood, where people just like me in so many ways, have a vastly different experience of life simply because they happen to be born in a country which is poor. It opened my eyes to the privileged position I had been born into, and to the responsibility that comes with it. It changed the way I wanted to live my life.

Action Guide

✔ *Get informed about the issues – the power of information*

Many forms of oppression and exploitation today are subtle and complex systems that rely on ignorance for their survival. It's so important that we get to grips with the issues. Then we can understand the root of the problems and help others understand the issues too. We'll also begin to understand what action we need to take.

Get informed about the issue by reading newspapers, magazines, books, publications and policy papers.

New Internationalist magazine reports on issues of world poverty and inequality. *Tearfund* provides free magazines for young people, students, youth leaders and adults containing information, campaign actions and urgent prayer needs for people, places and issues. *The Web* also contains a wealth of information on issues, countries, people groups, as well as movements to join and actions to take. See the directory for a fuller list of recommended books, magazines and websites.

Conferences and events. Find out what is happening locally and nationally to help you stay connected to the issues. Labour Behind the Label, the UK wing of the European Clean Clothes Campaign, holds open members meetings throughout the year, which are also open to interested members of the public. Some of these meetings involve garment industry workers from the developing world who speak about the issues they face.

Producer Tours. The Fairtrade Foundation organises producer tours around the UK and Ireland in the lead up to

Fairtrade Fortnight, which is the first two weeks in March each year. These tours are well worth looking out for, as they provide an excellent opportunity to hear first hand the experiences of farmers and producers from the developing world.

Courses. Find out which courses are most helpful for serving in particular areas and roles. The Web has information on academic courses that will help you deepen your understanding of theology and global issues.

☑ *Find out about organisations and agencies working to tackle poverty and injustice*

The Web. Search the Internet for organisations working in the areas you are interested in.

Mailing Lists. Get yourself onto the mailing list of organisations and agencies that will keep you informed on the issue. Most will be happy to send you free, regular news, prayer and campaign resources by post or email.

Offer support. Work out one practical way in which you can help, perhaps as a volunteer, a financial supporter, or as a pray-er for an organisation, network or local project working to tackle poverty or injustice. For international organisations and networks, the Web will have lists of the volunteer opportunities available, and the time commitment required. For local projects check out the volunteer bureau or Yellow Pages to see which projects are operating, and contact them directly to see what their volunteer needs are. Ask your church leader if they know what is already happening locally.

See the directory at the back of the book for suggested information sources and contact details.

☑ *Explore 'alternative' careers*

If you think God may be calling you to work for an agency, network or organisation that is seeking to alleviate poverty or tackle injustice, here are some practical steps that may be a helpful place to start:

Sign up for vacancy lists. Many organisations have email or postal vacancy updates that will inform you regularly about which job opportunities are available.

Volunteer. This can be an excellent way to find out more about an organisation you are interested in working for, and discover how you fit with their ethos and aims.

Send for the application pack. You may not be in a position to apply for a job right away, but a great way to find out more about a particular career is to sign up for the vacancy list, and when jobs come up that you might like to apply for in future, check out the requirements online if available, or send off for an application pack. (Remember to include a S.A.E to reduce cost.) This will tell you what the required qualifications, skills and experience for the role are.

Christian Vocations. This is an organisation that places Christians in jobs and voluntary positions all around the world. Their resources include an online programme to help match your skills and calling to a suitable job and location.

☑ *Get the lowdown on overseas teams and ethical tourism*

The Christian Vocations Short Term Directory is a great first place to start if you want to explore short-term gap year, summer activities, study options or insight trips. It's the most comprehensive directory of opportunities in short-term service with details of programmes in the UK and abroad. www.christianvocations.org

Connect with people who are, and have been, overseas. Many have prayer lists and newsletters that will give you a true insight into the reality of living and working in the developing world or elsewhere.

Transform. Tearfund's Transform programme sends teams overseas to work alongside their partners in one of over twenty countries, bringing help and hope to poorer communities. Teams range from two weeks, four to six weeks or four months, doing anything from practical work like painting and building, to caring for children. www.tearfund.org/transform

Ethical travel

Responsible Travel. This company enables you to book an ethical holiday that caters for all budgets and tastes including beach holidays, safaris and winter sports as well as a wide variety of locations. www.responsibletravel.com

The Good Alternative Travel Guide. This is a guidebook for responsible community-based tourism projects, offering hundreds of holidays.

Twenty

Lifestyle Habit 5: Committing Choices to God

'If we ignore the world we betray the word of God which sends us out to serve the world. If we ignore the word of God we have nothing to bring to the world.'
Micah Declaration

Intimacy With God That Impacts The Poor

Love the Lord your God with all your heart, all your soul, all your strength, and all your mind', and 'Love your neighbour as yourself' (Lk. 10:27).

Heart and soul

We are being called to love God with all of our hearts and souls. But what should that look like in our lifestyles? He is to be our all-consuming passion, he is to be what our heart longs for, and he is to be where we find our full satisfaction and happiness. We are called to love him with all our emotions, right to the core of our very being, and to 'fix our eyes on Jesus', as our first love.

As we do this, we will find that the love we have for the people around us will change and grow – as we look at them more and more through God's eyes. It is only the power of God's Holy Spirit moving in us, that will open our eyes to see people the way God wants us to see them. The more connected to God's heart we are, the more God will break our hearts for the things that break his. No matter how compelling a story, or shocking a statistic, we will never respond to our neighbours living in poverty the way God wants us to – unless our hearts break for the things that break his.

Helmut Thielecke said, 'Man becomes a holy thing, a neighbour, only if we realise that he is the property of God and that Jesus Christ died for him.'[58] God knows every one of the 1,200 billion people who will earn less than 60p today. He knows the names of the 246 million children who will go out to work instead of going to school today. [59] If we love God with all of our heart and soul, then the way we see our neighbours will reflect how he sees them. The way we treat them will reflect how he would treat them.

As his precious creation – not as an inconvenience.

As unique individuals – not as statistics.

As people to be treated with love and dignity – not to exploit and oppress.

As people with God-given potential to fulfil – not with a hopeless future.

Strength

If we are going to live lives of obedience to him, it will require all of our commitment. Submitting our will to his call on our lives will demand all the strength we've got.

No matter how moved we may feel when we see a documentary, hear a news report or read an article. No matter how many good intentions we have to do something to help, to write that letter, to give that money or even to pray about it, we all know that in our own strength very soon our good intentions can remain as just that – intentions. There will always be something more urgent to do, something that 'just can't wait'. There will always be a better time, when it's less busy, when we're less tired. There's always tomorrow or next week. But as we all know, tomorrow rarely, if ever, comes.

God became flesh and blood and moved into the neighbourhood.
The Message

When Jesus said to the disciples in the garden of Gethsemane that 'the spirit is willing but the flesh is weak' he could have been speaking it straight to us, today. It's so hard for us to live a life where we are truly loving our neighbour as we love ourselves because it is counter cultural. It is literally counter to, going against, the values, priorities and behaviour of our culture. It also goes against all our natural desires to please ourselves.

Psalm 73:26 says, 'My flesh and my heart may fail, but God is the strength of my heart and my portion forever.' We need God to give us the discipline and will to make lifestyle choices where we put others needs before our own. We need God to give us compassion and courage to want to speak up for those who most people ignore. We need God to remind us to pray and to act when we simply forget. We need God's strength to go against the flow when we begin to slip back into the world's mould. We need God to soften our hearts when we become apathetic.

On our own, our efforts will simply be like scooping water out of a shallow puddle – they'll very soon run dry. But if we draw on Jesus, the water of life, to refresh us, revitalise us and give us his reserves of love and compassion for others, then Isaiah 58 promises that we will become 'like a well watered garden. Like a spring whose waters will never run dry'. We will have a wellspring of love bubbling up within us, a never-ending supply to draw strength from and to pour out onto the neighbours who we are called to love.

Only God can give us the strength to live the life he calls us to.

Mind

Every day we are bombarded by images, messages and distractions vying for our attention. To be able to filter these messages, and separate the truth from the lies, requires us to fill our minds with the things of God. The more we keep soaking up God's word – the more it will open our eyes in fresh ways, showing us what steps and choices God wants us to take on our journey of life. The pages of the Bible simply ooze God's heart of love and compassion, and the more we get stuck into it, the more amazed we will be at how it begins to impact our mindset, our actions and what we value and long for.

Viv Grigg is a New Zealander who moved into a squatter settlement in the Philippines to live with and serve the people there. He wanted to preach good news as well as *be* good news to the poor by planting a church and help alleviate poverty. His ministry birthed a movement, which still exists today called Servant's to Asia's Urban Poor. He writes about what fired him up and kept him strong to live the lifestyle he was called to, in his book, *Companion to the Poor*:

> There can be little success here without the daily memorizing of the word of God until hundreds and indeed thousands of verses control our thinking. I can well

remember several Godly men, about whose lives I have
noticed an unusually toughened holiness. They were men
of the memorized word, men of Holy mind.[60]

Through soaking up God's word we will absorb something
of the character, heart and passion of our amazing Father.
For us to see our neighbours the way God sees them, we
must gaze into the eyes of the source of love and
compassion. It is only by living lives
of intimacy with God, where we are
learning from him, can we ever *'Reduce the distance*
begin to reflect him in our everyday *between yourself and the*
attitudes and choices. Prayer is *poor.' Richard Foster*
literally our lifeline in this. Stopping
and spending time in God's
presence to really seek his will, connect with his heart, and
hear what he is wanting from us – is something that will
transform us, freeing us up to serve, giving us the boldness
to take risks.

Viv Grigg writes,

> I easily get wiped out and discouraged unless each day I
> get that time with God, going over every attitude,
> meditating on each detail of life and praying over each step
> forward. If I do not spend that time, I will never have the
> dependence on God and humility to survive emotionally in
> this place, nor can God advance his kingdom.[61]

Bringing those who are facing poverty, injustice and
oppression before God and asking him to increase our
compassion and our love for them, will change our hearts
and the way we see our neighbours. Praying over streets,
cities, over nations, over issues is the only thing that will
bring the eternal change that is needed to transform lives.

We also need to come to God to simply listen to him – to wait on him, to create space for him to put people, or issues, or places or situations on our hearts and give us the courage to live it out. It is then that our lifestyle choices will change to reflect God's heart for justice and his passion for the poor.

If you have a bank account, you are part of the 8% wealthiest people in the world. Miniature Earth 2002

In Clayborne Carson's book, *The Autobiography of Martin Luther King Jr*, a section of King's journal tells of how prayer was literally his lifeline as he tried to obey God's call on his life to speak up on behalf of the black community, and stand up against injustice. He writes of a night, following a protest march when he had just received one of thirty or forty death threats, which were being directed at him on a daily basis.

King writes,

> And I got to the point where I just couldn't take it any longer. I was weak. Something said to me, 'you can't call on Daddy now; you can't even call on Mama. You've got to call on that something in that person that your daddy used to tell you about, that power that can make a way out of no way.' With my head in my hands I bowed over the kitchen table and prayed aloud. The words I spoke to God that midnight are still vivid in my memory. 'Lord, I'm down here trying to do what's right. I think I'm right. I am here taking a stand for what I believe is right. But Lord, I must confess that I'm weak now, I'm faltering. I'm losing my courage. Now, I'm afraid. And I can't let the people see me like this because if they see me weak and losing my courage, they will begin to get weak. The people are looking to me for leadership, and if I stand before them

without strength and courage, they too will falter. I am at the end of my powers. I have nothing left. I've come to the point where I can't face it alone.

It seemed as though I could hear the quiet voice of an inner assurance saying, 'Martin Luther stand up for righteousness. Stand up for justice. Stand up for truth. And Lo, I will be with you. Even until the end of the world.

I'll tell you I've seen the lightning flash. I've heard the thunder roar. I've felt sin breakers dashing trying to conquer my soul. But I heard the voice of Jesus saying still to fight on. He promised never to leave me alone.

At that moment I experienced the presence of the Divine as I have never experienced him before.

Almost at once my fears began to go. My uncertainty disappeared. I was ready to face anything.

References

1 *No Nonsense Guide to Fair Trade.* David Ransom/New Internationalist 2001.
2 HEED, Gender in Danger report, 2002 Bangladesh.
3 Liz Jennings, *Uncovered*, Tearfund, 2003.
4 Cafod, Fashion Victims Report
5 ILO Report 2000.
6 Clean Clothes Campaign.
7 ILO Report 2000.
8 *Mustard seed Vs McWorld,* Tom Sine, 2000
9 HEED, Bangladesh, 2002.
10 Labour Behind the Label *Wearing Thin* report 2001.
11 Labour Behind the Label *Wearing Thin* report 2001.
12 National Labour Committee.
13 International Textiles, Garment and Leather Workers Federation 2004.
14 Labour Behind the Label *Wearing Thin* report 2001.
15 Labour Behind the Label *Wearing Thin* report 2001.
16 ITGLWF 2004.
17 War on Want.
18 ITGLWF.
19 ITGLWF.
20 Clean Clothes Campaign report 2002.
21 Cafod, Fashion Victims Report.
22 London Fashion Week Report 2004.
23 Cafod, Fashion Victims Report.
24 ITGLWF 2004.
25 International Confederation of Free Trade Unions Report September 2003.
26 G. Moher 2003, recorded in Oxfam report *Trading Away Your Rights*.
27 *Uncovered*, Tearfund, 2002.
28 Oxfam *Trading Away Your Rights* Report 2004.
29 Fairtrade Foundation, *Spilling the Beans on the coffee trade*, 2002.
30 Day Chocolate Company, 2002.
31 Fairtrade Foundation.

32   Fairtrade Foundation, 2004.
33   Trade Justice Movement.
34   Oxfam, *Cultivating Poverty Report*, Sept 2002
35   Christian Aid, 2004.
36   London Fashion Week Report 2004.
37   Paul Tournier, quoted in *Love Beyond Reason* by John
     Ortberg p82 (Zondervan, 1998).
38   John Stott, *Issues Facing Christians Today* (London:
     Marshall Pickering, 1990), 19.
39   Fairtrade Foundation, 2004.
40   Fairtrade Foundation, 2004.
41   Fairtrade Foundation, 2004.
42   Fairtrade Foundation.
43   *Uncovered*, Tearfund, 2002.
44   Day Chocolate Company.
45   Fairtrade Foundation, 2004.
46   Fairtrade Foundation, 2004.
47   Day Chocolate Company.
48   London Fashion Week Report 2004.
49   *Uncovered*, Tearfund, 2004.
50   *Uncovered*, Tearfund, 2002.
51   Ronald J. Sider, *Rich Christians in an age of hunger*
     (London: Hodder & Stoughton, 1997).
52   *Uncovered*, Tearfund, 2002.
53   P. Dixon, *The Truth About Westminster: Can We Change the
     Heart of British Politics?* (Eastbourne: Kingsway, 1996).
54   Richard J. Foster, *Money, Sex and Power: The Challenge of
     the Disciplined Life* (Harper Collins, August 1987).
55   Statistics from *Miniature Earth* 2002.
56   Tim Chester, *Good News to the Poor* (Leicester: Inter-varsity
     Press, 2004). The figures quoted are taken from *Social
     Trends 33*, HMSO, 2003.
57   Liz Jennings, *Uncovered*, Tearfund, 2004.
58   Helmut Thielecke, quoted in *Quotes & Annecdotes* Anthony
     P. Castle (Kevin Mayhew Ltd, 1994).
59   International Labour Organisation.
60   Viv Gregg, *Companion to the Poor* (Oxford: Lion, 1985).
61   *Companion to the Poor*.

Directory

This information is accurate, to the best of our knowledge, at the time of print. For up-to-the-minute-information please visit the listed websites. This directory is by no means exhaustive – it is simply offered as a getting started guide for information and action. There are so many suppliers and organisations working in this area that it simply isn't possible to include them all. We would encourage you to search the Web to discover the wealth of information available. The authors are not responsible for the content of the suppliers, organisations, websites or resources included here.

Contents:

Books

Ethical Lifestyle

The No Nonsense Guide to Fairtrade
The human story behind the products we consume.
David Ransom
Published in association with New Internationalist by Verso

Ethical Shopping
Where to shop, what to buy and what to do to make a difference.
William Young and Richard Welford
Vision Paperbacks

The Good Shopping Guide
Ethical ratings for well known brands.
The Ethical Marketing Group

No Logo
Naomi Klein
Flamingo

L is for Lifestyle
Christian living that doesn't cost the earth.
Ruth Valerio
Inter Varsity Press

The Good Alternative Travel Guide
Mark Mann
2002 Tourism Concern/Earthscan

Simplicity, Love and Justice
A Discussion Course Manual
James Odgers and Ruth Valerio
Alpha International

God's Heart for the Poor

Good News about Injustice:
A Witness of Courage in a Hurting World.
Gary A. Haugen
Inter Varsity Press

What if You Got Involved?
Taking a stand against social injustice.
Graham Gordon
Paternoster Press

God of the poor
A Biblical Vision of God's Present Rule.
Dewi Hughes with Matthew Bennett
OM Publishing

Rich Christians in an Age of Hunger
What can be done about the imbalances of poverty and
wealth in our world?
Ron Sider
Hodder and Stoughton

Good News to the Poor
Sharing the Gospel through social involvement.
Tim Chester
Inter Varsity Press

Prayer

Operation World
A comprehensive guide to praying for the nations.
Patrick Johnstone and Jason Mandryck
Paternoster Publishing

Fairtrade

Fairtrade Foundation
Room 204,16 Baldwin's Gardens
London
EC1N 7RJ
Tel: 02074055942
mail@fairtrade.org.uk
www.fairtrade.org.uk

Websites

Banana link
www.bananalink.org.uk

European Fairtrade Association
www.eftafairtrade.org

Fairtrade Federation US
www.fairtradefederation.org

Fairtrade Labelling Organisations International
www.fairtrade.net

Fairtrade Products

Fresh Fruit

Fairtrade apples: Tesco
Fairtrade bananas: Co-op, Sainsbury's and Waitrose stores, most branches of Safeway, Asda, Somerfield, Tesco and Budgens, and organic food stores.
Fairtrade mangoes: Co-op, Sainsbury's, Waitrose and Tesco
Fairtrade oranges: Co-op and Tesco
Fairtrade pineapples: Co-op, Somerfield, Tesco and Waitrose

Coffee

Brian Wogan Fairtrade Costa Rica Ground Coffee in beans or ground, dark or light roast:
Delicatessens and health food stores or online at www.wogan-coffee.co.uk

Cafédirect 5065 and Organic Decaffeinated Freeze Dried Coffee, Decaffeinated Ground Coffee, Medium Roast Ground Coffee, Rich Roast Ground Coffee, Organic Full Roast Ground Coffee, Kilimanjaro Mountain Special Ground Coffee and Organic Machu Picchu Mountain Special Fresh Ground Coffee:
Major supermarkets, independent retailers, Oxfam shops, Traidcraft mail order and online shopping, One World shops and independent health food and wholefood stores. A Cafédirect Espresso Coffee is also available in Costa Coffee shops.

Clipper Organic Instant Granules, Organic Freeze Dried Decaffeinated, American Style Organic Roast and Ground

Arabica, French Style Organic Roast and Ground Arabica, Italian Style Organic Roast and Ground Arabica, Espresso Organic Roast and Ground Arabica, Decaffeinated Roast and Ground Arabica:
Most major supermarkets and independent shops.

Coffeehouse Fairtrade Colombian Excelso Coffee, Tanzania Kilimanjaro Arabica Coffee, Tanzania Screen Robusta Coffee, Costa Rica Coffee, Peru "Titicaca" Coffee, Honduras Coffee, Nicaragua Coffee, Guatemala Coffee. Fairtrade Organic Ethiopia Sidamo Coffee, Ethiopia Djimma Coffee, Costa Rica Coffee, Sumatra Mandheling Coffee, Swiss Water Decaffeinated Coffee, Sumatra Mandheling Coffee, Honduras Coffee:
Independent shops.

Co-op Own Brand Instant Fair Trade Coffees: Medium Roast Granules, Rich Roast Granules, Rich Roast Decaffeinated, Gold Roast Freeze Dried, Gold Roast Freeze Dried Decaffeinated and Organic Freeze Dried. Own Brand Fair Trade Ground Coffees, Original Ground, Decaffeinated Ground, After Dinner Ground, Colombian Ground, Italian Ground, Organic Ground, American Style Organic Roast and Ground Arabica, French Style Organic Roast and Ground Arabica, Italian Style Organic Roast and Ground Arabica, Espresso Organic Roast and Ground Arabica and Decaffeinated Organic Roast and Ground Arabica:
Co-op stores.

Essential Organic Fairtrade Mexican Roast and Ground Coffee and Organic Fairtrade Guatemalan Roast and Ground Coffee:
Health food and independent shops.

Equal Exchange Organic Medium Roast Ground Coffee, Organic Dark Roast Ground Coffee and Organic Decaffeinated Ground Coffee, Organic Espresso Blend Coffee, Sumatran Takegon Ground Coffee, Colombian Excelso Ground Coffee, Organic Ethiopian Limu Coffee and Beans, Organic Decaffeinated Coffee Beans, Organic Dark Roast Coffee Beans, Organic Medium Roast Coffee Beans:
Health food and whole food shops, and by mail order from Equal Exchange.

Essential Fairtrade Mexican Roast and Ground Coffee and Fairtrade Guatemalan Roast and Ground Coffee:
Essential.

Ferrari's Fairtrade Espresso Blend, Cafetiere Blend, Pour & Serve and Decaffeinated Espresso Beans & Ground:
Independent shops.

Johnson's Costa Rica Fairtrade Blend Ground Coffee:
Sainsbury's and Co-op stores in Northern Ireland.

Percol Colombia Ground Coffee, Guatemala Organic Ground Coffee, Latin American Organic Ground Coffee, Nicaragua Ground Coffee, Organic Americano and Organic Espresso Ground Coffee:
Major supermarkets, independent retailers and health food stores.

Pret-A-Manger Filter Coffee: Majority of Pret-A-Manger stores.

Rombouts Fairtrade Organic Individual Filter Coffees:
Sainsbury's, Safeway and Tesco stores.

Sainsbury's Own Brand Fairtrade Colombian Fresh Roast Ground Coffee and Decaffeinated Fairtrade Colombian Fresh Roast Ground Coffee. *Somerfield Own Brand* Fairtrade Colombian Roast and Ground Coffee.

Starbucks Own Brand 'Coffee of the day' (cafétière) once a month in all Starbucks coffee shops. Own brand Fairtrade Coffee Beans are also in Starbucks coffee shops.

Suma Organic Dark Roast Coffee, Organic Decaffeinated Coffee, Organic Expresso Blend Coffee and Organic , Medium Roast Coffee:
Health and whole food shops.

Tesco Own Brand Fair trade Roast and Ground Coffee, Fair trade Decaffeinated Ground Coffee, Fair trade Instant Freeze Dried Coffee:
Most Tesco stores.

Traidcraft Organic Dark Roast, Medium Roast and Organic and Decaffeinated Roast Ground Coffees:
Whole food shops and by mail order and online shopping from Traidcraft.

Union Coffee Roasters Organic Mexico, Organic Natural Spirit and Rwanda Cafe Maraba Bourbon Roast Ground Coffee: Sainsbury's and independent shops.

Tea

Clipper Fairtrade Tea Bags, Fairtrade Loose Tea and Fairtrade Green Teas with Echinacea, Ginkgo or Ginseng, Organic Green Tea with Aloe Vera, Green Tea with Lemon, Organic Chamomile Tea, Organic Peppermint Tea, Organic

Black Chai Tea, Organic Earl Grey 50's Tea, Organic Early Grey Loose Tea, Organic English Breakfast 40's Tea, Organic English Breakfast Loose Tea, Organic Lapsang Souchong 50's Tea, Organic Lapsang Souchong Loose Tea, Organic Darjeeling 50's Tea, Organic Darjeeling Loose Tea, Organic Assam 50's Tea, Organic Assam Loose Tea, Organic Ceylon 50's Tea:
Mail order from Clipper. See www.clipper-teas.com

Equal Exchange Organic Assam Tea Bags and Loose Tea, Organic Breakfast Tea Bags and Loose Tea, Organic Earl Grey Tea Bags and Loose Tea, Organic Darjeeling Tea Bags and Loose Tea, Organic Green Tea Bags and Loose Tea, Organic Lemon Green Tea Bags, Organic Masala Chai Tea Bags, Organic Mint Green Tea Bags, Organic Premium Tea Bags, Organic Rooibos Tea:
Health food and wholefood shops, delicatessens and by mail order from Equal Exchange.

Hampstead Tea & Coffee Company Organic Biochai Masala Leaf Tea and Tea Bags, First Flush Leaf Tea, Makaibari Darjeeling Leaf Tea, Green Leaf Tea and Tea Bags, Oolong Leaf Tea, Earl Grey Tea Bags and Leaf Tea, Ginger Green Tea Bags, Green Verveine Tea Bags and White Leaf Tea:
Specialist shops and by mail order from Hampstead (020 8731 9833).

Imporient (UK) Ltd Catering Fairtrade Tea Bags and Tagged Tea Bags and Loose (Leaf) Tea:
Independent shops and from Imporient tea@imporient.com

Morrisons Fair Trade Organic Tea Bags.

Sainsburys Own Brand Fairtrade Tea.

Somerfield Own Brand Fairtrade Tea.

Steenbergs Limited Organic Assam Tea, Organic Ceylon Tea, Organic Darjeeling Tea, Organic Earl Grey Tea, Organic Green Tea: Independent health food shops.

Suma Organic Assam Tea Bags, Organic Earl Grey Tea Bags, Organic Darjeeling Tea Bags and Organic Breakfast Blend Tea Bags: Health and wholefood shops.

Teadirect Tea Bags, Organic Earl Grey Tea Bags and Organic Green Tea Bags with Lemongrass or Cinnamon: Major supermarkets, independent retailers, Oxfam shops, *Traidcraft* mail order, One World shops and independent health and whole food stores. Tea bags available in Costa Coffee shops.

Traidcraft Indian Ocean Tea Bags, East African Gold Tea Bags, One Cup English Breakfast Tea Bags, One Cup East Africa Tea Bags, One Cup Earl Grey Tea Bags, Tanzanian Loose Tea:
Wholefood and One World shops, and by mail order and online shopping from Traidcraft.

Sugar

Equal Exchange Organic Raw Cane Sugar: Health food shops and by mail order from Equal Exchange.

Co-op Own Brand Fair Trade White Granulated Sugar, Fair Trade Golden Granulated Sugar.

Traidcraft Organic Raw Cane Sugar: Health-food and wholefood shops, mail order and online shopping from Traidcraft.

Whitworths Granulated Sugar, Golden Granulated Sugar, Demerara Sugar: Tesco and Budgens stores.

Fruit Juices

JP Juices JP Orange Juice: Co-op, Sainsbury's and Tesco stores.

Fruit Passion Orange, Tropical and Breakfast Juices: Co-op, Tesco, Sainsbury's, Somerfield, Safeway, Asda and Waitrose stores.

Tesco Own Brand Fair trade Orange Juice.

Honey

Cotswold Swallows set or clear Fairtrade Honey: Oxfam shops and by mail order.

Equal Exchange set or clear Organic Honey: Wholefood shops and by mail order.

Rowse Fairtrade Pure Natural Chilean Honey: Independent and wholefood shops.

Traidcraft Fairtrade set or clear Chilean Honey: Traidcraft mail order.

Snacks

Alara Wholefoods Fairtrade Muesli: Wholefood and independent shops.

Co-op Own Brand Fair Trade Chocolate Cake, All Butter Chocolate Chip Shortbread Biscuits, Muesli, Easter Chocolate Ring Cake, Four Chocolate Brownies.

Dove Farm Foods Fairtrade Milk Chocolate Organic Biscuits: Budgens, Waitrose, Booths and health food stores.

Equal Exchange Plain Chocolate Coated Brazil Nuts: Some Sainsbury's and wholefood shops and by mail order from Equal Exchange.

Tesco Own Brand Fair trade Muesli, Fair trade Double Chocolate Chip Cookies.

Traidcraft Apricot Geobar, Cranberry and Raisin Geobar and Chocolate Geobar Snack Bars: Waitrose, Sainsbury's, Safeway, Tesco, Co-op, Booths supermarkets, Oxfam shops, and mail order and online shopping from Traidcraft. Organic Brazil Nut Cookies, Double Chocolate Chip Cookies and Stem Ginger Cookies:
Sainsbury's, wholefood shops and by mail order and online shopping from Traidcraft.
Traidcraft Chocolate Beans, Chocolate Brazil Nuts, Chocolate Ginger, Chocolate Honeycomb, Chocolate Peanuts, Chocolate Raisins and Chocolate Mini Eggs: Fair Trade shops, world shops, and by mail order and online shopping from Traidcraft.

Tropical Wholefoods Banana and Honey Fairtrade Bar, Apricot and Kernal Fairtrade Bar, Mango and Brazil Fairtrade Bar, Pineapple and Cashew Bars:
Fair trade shops, health and whole food shops, mail order and online shopping from www.tropicalwholefoods.co.uk

Village Bakery Organic Christmas Pudding, Christmas Cake, Brandy Butter Shortbread and Fireside Cookies. Available on a seasonal basis in Oxfam shops and independent shops, and online at www.village-bakery.com

Chocolate

Chocaid Fine Swiss Organic Milk Chocolate, Extra Dark
Organic Swiss Chocolate, Champagne Truffles, Orange
Truffles, Mint Truffles:
Chocaid and Budgens.

Co-op Own brand Fairtrade Milk Chocolate, Fairtrade
Crispy Milk Chocolate, Fairtrade Dark Chocolate, Fairtrade
Fruit and Nut Chocolate, Fairtrade Hollow Milk Chocolate
Easter Egg, Easter Hunt Egg, Easter Ring Cake.

The Day Chocolate Company Divine Milk Chocolate,
Dubble Milk Chocolate Crispy Crunch Bar, Darkly Divine
Plain Chocolate, Divine Milk Chocolate with Hazelnuts,
Divine White Chocolate, Divine Coffee White Chocolate,
Divine Orange Milk Chocolate, Divine Milk Chocolate
Eggs. www.divinechocolate.com
Divine Milk Chocolate:
Asda, Booths, Co-op, Morrisons, Sainsbury's, Somerfield,
BAFTS, NUS stores, health food and wholefood shops.
Dubble Milk Chocolate Crispy Crunch Bar: Asda, Bells
Stores, Blockbuster Video, Booths, Co-op, Iceland,
Jacksons, Safeway, Sainsbury's, Spar, Tesco, Waitrose,
Whistlestops and in independent shops, garage forecourts,
leisure outlets and NUS stores.
Darkly Divine Plain Chocolate, Divine Milk Chocolate
with Hazelnuts, Divine White Chocolate, Divine Coffee
White Chocolate and Divine Orange Milk Chocolate:
Waitrose with other major supermarkets following soon;
health and wholefood shops.

Green & Black's Maya Gold Organic Chocolate and Maya
Gold Organic Chocolate Easter Egg: Most major
supermarkets and health food stores.

Starbucks Milk Chunky Chocolate, Dark Chunky Chocolate, White Chunky Chocolate: Starbucks.

Tesco Own Brand Fairtrade Milk Chocolate Bar and Fairtrade Dark Chocolate Bar.

Traidcraft chocolate bar range. Includes Organic Milk, Plain, Cappuccino and Praline Chocolate and bars of Almond White, Honey Milk Chocolate and Rico Milk Chocolate Bars with filled centre:
Traidcraft mail order and online shopping from Traidcraft, One World and wholefood shops.
Boxed Milk and Plain Chocolates with filled centres:
Traidcraft mail order and online shopping and from One World shops.

Jams and Spreads

Duerr's Fairtrade Orange Marmalade, Strawberry Conserve: Tesco stores.

Traidcraft Organic Fairtrade Strawberry Jam, Organic Fairtrade Seville Orange Marmalade, Organic Fairtrade Chocolate Hazelnut Spread: Traidcraft online.

Shaws of Huddersfield Make a Difference Cranberry Sauce, Apple Sauce, Mango Chutney: Independent shops.

Geo Organics Mango Chutney: Sainsbury's, Tesco and independent shops.

Roses

Fairtrade roses are sold at Tesco.

Footballs

Fairtrade footballs available as Footballs Direct Standard Ball and Footballs Direct match quality FIFA Ball: Co-op stores and www.fairdealtrading.co.uk

Fairtrade Hampers

Fair Trade Direct
www.fairtradehampers.co.uk
Wedding, new baby, special occasion and treat hampers.

This is a complete list at the time of writing. To keep up to date on new Fairtrade ranges, go to
www.fairtrade.org.uk/products.htm

Mail order and online shopping is available from:
Equal Exchange
Tel: 0131 220 3484
www.equalexchange.co.uk

Traidcraft
Tel: 0191 491 0591
www.traidcraft.co.uk

Clipper
Tel: 0800 169 3552
www.clipper-teas.com

Tearcraft
Tel: 0870 240 4896
www.tearcraft.org

Ethical Trade

Information Websites

Ethical Trading Initiative UK
www.ethicaltrade.org

CORE
The Corporate Responsibility Coalition
www.corporate-responsibility.org

Ethical Consumer Research Association
www.ethicalconsumer.org

The International Federation for Alternative Trade (IFAT)
www.ifat.org

Ethical Outlets - General

Here is a list of shops and online stores, which either sell
fairly traded goods or ethical goods. 'Fair Trade' goods
mean that they are signed up to a strict code of trading,
guaranteeing a fair wage and safe, healthy working
conditions. The term 'Ethical' is very broad here, but in a
basic sense means that they take into account
environmental and social justice issues.

Ethical Junction
www.ethical-junction.org
A vast array of ethical suppliers and retailers.

Ethical Shopper
www.ethicalshopper.co.uk
An ethical alternative to your everyday shopping.

Fairtradeonline
www.fairtradeonline.com
An Oxfam and Traidcraft marketplace.

Get Ethical
www.getethical.com
An extensive website for buying ethical and green products.

Tearcraft
www.tearcraft.org
The Fair Trade catalogue of Tearfund.

Traidcraft
www.traidcraft.co.uk
Sells a wide range of Fair Trade goods.

Fashion

American Apparel
www.americanapparel.co.uk
Trendy 'blank' T-shirts and other clothing.

CRED Foundation
www.cred.tv
Fair Trade jewellery and goods.

Epona Sportswear Company
www.eponasport.com
A new kind of sportswear. Fair Trade and Organic.

Ethically me
www.ethicallyme.com
Stylish ranges for all seasons.

Ethical Threads
www.ethicalthreads.co.uk
Wholesale ethical T-shirts for music and concert
merchandising.

Ethical Wares
www.ethicalwares.com
An ethically-based mail order company.

Fair Trade South Africa
www.fairtradesouthafrica.com
Helps small South African fashion and craft enterprises to
sell overseas.

Ganesha
www.ganesha.co.uk
Quality clothes, accessories and home furnishings.

Get Ethical
www.getethical.com
Extensive website with clothes, food and more.

Gossypium
www.gossypium.co.uk
Organic and Fairtrade cotton clothes and home textiles.

Hug
www.hug.co.uk
Organic Fair Trade clothes.

Marlo Clothing
www.marlo.co.uk
Fair Trade organic cotton and hemp clothing.

Natural Collection
www.naturalcollection.com
Hemp clothing, organic exercise gear, organic t-shirts.

No Sweat
Nosweatapparel.com
T-shirts, sweatshirts, jeans and women's athletic wear.

People Tree Ltd
www.ptree.co.uk
Funky organic, Fair Trade clothes, jewellery and other accessories.

Ralper
www.ralper.co.uk
Trendy Fair Trade clothes.

Silverchilli.com
www.silverchilli.com
Fair Trade silver jewellery.

Smile Child
Smilechild.co.uk
Offers a full range of Fair Trade and organic clothes, toys, toiletries and eco-nappies.

Sweatx
www.sweatx.net
Mainly T-shirts, shorts and headwear.

British Association of Fair Trade Shops

British Association of Fair Trade Shops
BAFTS is a network of independent Fair Trade shops or
World shops across the UK.
info@bafts.org.uk
Website: www.bafts.org.uk

East Anglia
Colchester
Traders Fair World Shop
Portal Precinct, Sir Isaac's Walk, Colchester, CO1 1JJ
Tel 01206 763380
foxnorth@tinyworld.co.uk

Norwich
The World Shop
NEAD, 38 Exchange St, Norwich, NR2 1AX
Tel 01603 610993
www.nead.org.uk

St Ives
Just Sharing
The Free Church (URC), Market Hill, St Ives, Huntingdon,
PE27 5AL
Tel 01480 496570

South West
Barnstaple
Chandni Chowk
102 Boutport St, Barnstaple, EX31 1SY
Tel 01271 374714
www.chandnichowk.co.uk

Bath
Chandni Chowk
6 New Bond St Place, Bath, BA1 1BH
Tel 01225 484700
www.chandnichowk.co.uk

Bradford-on-Avon
Bishopston Trading Company
33 Silver St, Bradford-on-Avon, BA15 2LB
Tel 01225 867485
www.bishopstontrading.co.uk

Bristol
Bishopston Trading Company
193 Gloucester Rd, Bishopston, Bristol, BS7 8BG
Tel 0117 9245598
Fax 0117 975 3590
info@bishopstontrading.co.uk
www.bishopstontrading.co.uk

Chandni Chowk
66 Park St, Bristol, BS1 5JN
Tel 0117 9300059
www.chandnichowk.co.uk

Exeter
Chandni Chowk
1 Harlequins, Paul Street, Exeter, EX4 3TT
Tel 01392 410201
www.chandnichowk.co.uk

Glastonbury
Bishopston Trading Company
8a High Street, Glastonbury, BA6 8SU
Tel 01458 83 5386
www.bishopstontrading.co.uk

Just Traiding
7 Fountain St, Nailsworth, Stroud, GL6 OBL
Tel 01453 833002

Nailsworth
Fair Oasis
9 Fountain Street, Nailsworth, Stroud, GL6 OBL
Tel 01453 833002

Stroud
Bishopston Trading Company
33 High Street, Stroud, GL5 1AJ
Tel 01453 766355
www.bishopstontrading.co.uk

Taunton
Chandni Chowk
14a, The Bridge, Riverside Place, Taunton, TA1 1UG
Tel 01823 327377
www.chandnichowk.co.uk

Totnes
Bishopston Trading Company
79 High Street, Totnes, TQ9 5PB
Tel 01803 86 8488
www.bishopstontrading.co.uk

Wimborne
Third World Crafts
8 Crown Mead, Wimborne, BH21 1ED
Tel 01202 849898

Midlands
Ashbourne
Pachacuti
19 Dig Street, Ashbourne, DE6 1GF
Tel 01335 300003
www.panamas.co.uk

Birmingham
Shared Earth
87 New St, Birmingham, B2 4BA
Tel 0121 6330151
www.sharedearth.co.uk

Cheltenham
One Village
First Floor, Regent Arcade, Cheltenham
Tel 0845 45847030
www.onevillage.co.uk

Rugby
World of Difference
20 High St, Rugby, CV21 3BG
Tel 01788 579191

Wirksworth
Traid Links
20 Market Place, Wirksworth, DE4 4ET
Tel 01629 824393
www.traid-links.co.uk

North East
Alnwick
A World of Difference
13 Narrowgate, Alnwick, NE66 1JH
Tel 01665 606005
www.aworldofdifference.co.uk

Berwick Upon Tweed
The Green Shop
30 Bridge St, Berwick Upon Tweed, TD15 1AQ
Tel 01289 305566

Durham
Gateway World Shop
Market Place, Durham, DH1 3NJ
Tel 0191 384 7173
www.gatewayworldshop.co.uk

Haworth
Sonia's Smile
85 Main St, Haworth, BD22 8DA
Tel 01535 647776
www.soniassmile.com

Hull
Hull One World Shop
c/o Central Methodist Hall, Waltham Street, King Edward
St, Hull HU1 3SQ
Tel 01482 327727
www.oneworldhull.co.uk

Leeds
Shared Earth
86 The Merrion Centre, Leeds, LS2 8PJ
Tel 0113 2426424
www.sharedearth.co.uk

Middlesbrough
Traidcraft
17 Corporation Rd (next to Clinkards, Middlesbrough),
TS1 1LW
Only during December

Shared Earth
1 Minster Gates, York, YO1 7HL
Tel 01904 632896
www.sharedearth.co.uk

Sheffield
Traidcraft Shop
142 Devonshire St, Sheffield, S3 7SF
Tel 0114 2726455

Stockton on Tees
North-South Trading
Stockton on Tees area, ring for details:
Tel 01740 630475

York
Fairer World
84 Gillygate, York, YO31 7EQ
Tel 01904 655116
fairerworld@aol.com

South East & London
Canterbury
Siesta
1 Palace St, Canterbury, CT1 2DY
Tel 01227 464614
www.siestacrafts.co.uk

Diversity
19 Church Lane, Leytonshire, London, E11 1HG
Tel 020 8539 4196

Ganesha
3 Gabriel's Wharf, 56 Upper Ground, London, SE1 9PP
Tel 020 7928 3444
www.ganesha.co.uk

Isle of Wight
Traidcraft Shop
119 School Green Rd, Freshwater, IOW, PO40 9AZ
Tel 01983 752451

London
Bag Lady
29 Webbs Road, London, SW11 6RU
Tel 020 7223 6800
www.gurushop.co.uk

One World Shop (Waterloo)
St John's Church, Waterloo Road, London, SE1 8TY
Tel 020 7401 8909

Oxford
Tumi
1/2 Little Clarendon St, Oxford, OX1 2HJ
Tel 01865 512307
www.tumicrafts.com

Paper High
Market Hall, Bottom Floor, Camden Lock Market,
London, N1
Tel 07734 104297
www.paperhigh.com

Reading
The World Shop
RISC, 35-39 London St, Reading, Berks, RG1 4PS
Tel 0118 958 6692
www.risc.org.uk

Woodstock
One Village
On the A44 at Woodstock, nr Oxford
Tel 0845 45847020
www.onevillage.co.uk

Scotland

Balmore
The Coach House
Balmore, nr Torrance, Glasgow, G64 4AE
Tel 01360 620742

Edinburgh
Hadeel
1 St Georges West Church Centre, 58 Shandwick Place,
Edinburgh EH2 4RT
Tel 0131 225 1922
palcrafts@fish.co.uk

One World Shop (Edinburgh)
St John's Church, Princes St, Edinburgh, EH2 4BJ
Tel 0131 2294541
www.oneworldshop.co.uk

Fife
Fair Shares
128 High Street, Burntisland, Fife KY3 9AP
Tel 07952 161305
fairshares@breathemail.net

Glasgow
One World Shop (Glasgow)
100 Byres Road, Glasgow, GL2 8TB
Tel 0141 357 1567
www.oneworldshop.co.uk

North Berwick
Earth Matters
67 High St, North Berwick, EH39 5NZ
Tel 01620 895401
www.earthmatters.co.uk

Paisley
Rainbow Turtle
7 Gauze Street, Paisley, PA1 1EP
Tel 0141 887 1881
rainbow-turtle@btopenworld.com

Wales

Cardiff
Fair Do's/Siopa Teg
10 Llandaff Rd, Canton, Cardiff, CF11 9NJ
Tel 029 20 222066
www.fairdos.com

Shared Earth
14/16 Royal Arcade, Cardiff, CF10 1AE
Tel 029 20 396900
www.sharedearth.co.uk

Conwy
Just Shopping
13 Bangor Rd, Conwy, LL32 8NG
Tel 07720 894023
www.justshopping.co.uk

News and Information

Magazines

Tearfund
Free magazines with prayer and action information on global issues:

Activist:	young people (11-17)
Uncovered:	students and young adults (18-22)
Teartimes:	for adults
Network:	for youth leaders
To subscribe:	Email: enquiry@tearfund.org
	Tel: 0845 355 8355 (ROI 0845 355 8355)

New Consumer Magazine
www.new-consumer.co.uk
Subscribe online or call 0141 335 9050.

Fair Comment
Fairtrade Foundation Magazine.
www.fairtrade.org.uk
Subscribe online or call 020 7405 5942.

Ethical Consumer Magazine
www.ethicalconsumer.org
Subscribe online or call 0161 226 2929.

New Internationalist Magazine
www.newint.org
Subscribe online or call 01865 811400.

Policy Reports

There are many excellent pamphlets and papers available from the following organisations, however it is best to contact them and ask them directly for their most up to date publications on this issue.

Tearfund Research and Policy reports
www.tearfund.org/campaigning

Oxfam Policy Report 'Trading Away Our Rights'
www.maketradefair.com
Report on women working in global supply chains.

Websites

Ethical Performance Newsletter
www.ethicalperformance.com

Natural Resources and Ethical Trade Programme
www.nri.org/NRET/

Oneworld
www.oneworld.net

Institutions and Organisations

Department for International Development, UK
www.dfid.gov.uk

European Commission – Trade
www.europa.eu.int/comm/trade/index_en.htm

International Labour Organisation
www.ilo.org

United Nations
www.un.org

United Nations Development Program
www.undp.org

World Trade Organisation
www.wto.org

International Standards

SA8000
www.cepaa.org

UN Global Compact
www.unglobalcompact.org

Fairtrade Mark UK
www.fairtrade.org.uk

RUGMARK
www.rugmark.net

The Good Shopping Guide
www.thegoodshoppingguide.co.uk

Organisations active on the garment industry

Ethical Trading Initiative
2nd Floor, Cromwell House
14 Fulwood Place, London WCIV 6HZ
Tel 020 7404 1463
Email eti@eti.org.uk
Website www.ethicaltrade.org

SOMO (Centre for Research on Multinational Corporations)
Keizersgracht 132 1015 CW
Amsterdam
Tel 00 3120 639 1291
Email somo@xs4all.nl

Campaigning on the garment industry

Tearfund
Lift the Label Campaign
100 Church Road, Teddington, Middlesex, TW11 8QE
Tel 0845 355 8355
ROI 0044 845 355 8355
enquiry@tearfund.org
To find out about Tearfund's Lift the Label ethical lifestyle
campaign, visit www.tearfund.org/liftthelabel

Tearfund's youth prayer and campaigns networks:
student net: for students and young adults (18-22)
youth net: for young people (11-17)
network engage: for youth leaders

Members receive regular email action updates giving
prayer and campaign actions on the Lift the Label ethical
lifestyle campaign plus Tearfund's debt, sustainable living

and trade campaigns. To subscribe email
enquiry@tearfund.org or visit www.tearfund.org/youth

Tearfund globalaction
Highlights key campaigning opportunities through a
quarterly publication, with additional email news, updates
and emergency action requests.
To join globalaction visit
www.tearfund.org/campaigning/globalaction

Trade Justice Movement
www.tradejusticemovement.org
Campaigning to make international trade rules work
better for the poor.

Labour Behind the Label
c/o NEAD, 38 Exchange St, Norwich NR2 1AX
Tel 01603 610 993
lbl@gn.apc.org
www.labourbehindthelabel.org

Clean Clothes Campaign
PO Box 115841001, GN Amsterdam
Tel 00 3120 412 2785
info@cleanclothes.org
www.cleanclothes.org

War on Want
Fenner Brockway House, 37-39 Great Guildford Street
London, SE1 0ES
Tel 020 7620 1111
mailroom@waronwant.org
www.waronwant.org

Oxfam
274 Banbury Road, Oxford, OX2 7DZ
Tel 0870 333 2700
oxfam@oxfam.org.uk
www.oxfam.org.uk

Women Working Worldwide
CER, Rm 126 Humanities Building, Rosamond St West
Manchester, M15 6LL
Tel 0161 247 1760
women-ww@MCR1.poptel.org.uk
www.poptel.org.uk/women-ww/

Behind the Label
www.behindthelabel.org
Online campaign resources and newsletter.

Working Conditions/Human Rights

Anti Slavery UK
www.antislavery.org

Global March Against Child Labour UK
www.globalmarch.org

National Labour Committee US
www.nlcnet.org

Ethical Banking

Co-operative Bank
www.co-operativebank.co.uk

Triodos Bank
www.triodos.co.uk

smile
www.smile.co.uk

EIRIS
www.eiris.org
An independent research provider for socially responsible
investors. Provides a directory of financial advisors who
specialise in ethical investment.

The UK Social Investment Forum
www.uksif.org
Promotes and encourages socially responsible investment
in the UK.

Travel and Tourism

Tourism Concern
www.tourismconcern.org.uk

Responsible Travel
www.responsibletravel.com

Christian Vocations
www.christianvocations.org

Tearfund Transform Teams
www.tearfund.org/transform

Environmental

Tearfund's Whose Earth? Campaign
www.tearfund.org/whoseearth
Sustainable Living Guide and resources with prayer and
campaign ideas to help the poor have access to
environmental resources and protection from the impact
of increasing disasters. It has been beyond the scope of
this book to explore the very important issue of the impact
our choices have on the environment, and in turn on the
poor. This website will explain the issues and point you to
further information and ideas for action.